Luminous Night's Journey

Luminous Night's Journey

An Autobiographical Fragment

A.H. Almaas

Diamond Books Berkeley, California

Cover photo: NASA/courtesy of World Perspectives, San Rafael, CA.

Cover design: Chris Molé

First published in 1995 by
Diamond Books
Almaas Publications
P.O. Box 10114
Berkeley, CA 94709

Second printing: 1996

ISBN 0-936713-08-9

Library of Congress Card Catalog Number: 96-084412

Typeset in 11 point Utopia by Byron Brown

Printed in the United States by
Malloy Lithographing

Dedicated
with love and gratitude to
my father, my mother and my grandmother
who raised me with such caring
that I learnt easily to trust reality,
and to be open to its mysteries.

Table of Contents

Introduction and Acknowledgments

This book follows a particular thread in the process of self-realization. Each chapter describes a self-contained segment of this process. Thus even though the book as a whole consists of one thread, each chapter is independent. The thread that runs through all the chapters is a chain of processes and experiences I have gone through personally, and selected for this book out of a much larger field of experience. I chose this particular thread partly because of my personal interest in reviewing it, and partly because it illuminates a process rarely discussed in spiritual literature.

Most serious spiritual writings focus on the process of realization of true nature, the absolute or divine essence. This is the ultimate nature and source of ourselves and of everything. The thread I follow in this book sheds light on the obscure process of how the soul, the individual consciousness, becomes integrated into this absolute nature, as and after the source of all experience is realized. I want to relate my experience and understanding of the fact that individual consciousness does not merely die away or get discarded, and to describe how it becomes clarified and integrated. This integration turns out to be the process through which the absolute manifests as an individual human being who embodies this ultimate truth in a personal life in the world.

I began this writing as my own personal contemplation, with a desire to explore this process in the form of creative writing. I was not thinking of publishing. I selected entries from my journal, which are mainly succinct and disconnected notes, and rewrote them in detail, fleshing out the nuances of my experience. In the course of this writing I agreed to give some public lectures, and decided to read some of this material as the subject of these lectures, with commentaries and clarifications. I viewed this approach as an experiment, for it is new for me to talk about my personal experience of spiritual realization in public. I did not know whether such public discussion of personal experience would have much value for the listeners. The response was so consistently positive, with feedback about its usefulness for many individuals, that I finally thought of publishing these writings as a book.

The process of my personal opening and transformation began many years before the experiences related in this book. This transformation has been a continual process of revelation of Being, our true nature, in various qualities and dimensions, accompanied by the development of a body of understanding of these manifestations and their relation to the experience of the ego self. These processes, experiences, realizations and insights have formed the major source of the teaching I have formulated, the Diamond Approach, which is the teaching of the Ridhwan School. I think that this book will provide at least a taste of the realizations and their associated processes that generated this body of knowledge, and will also provide a glimpse of how the Diamond Approach works.

I am indebted to many individuals and teachings for my personal transformation and continuing learning. The true source of my personal transformation and realization is Being itself, and its essential guidance. Yet I doubt that this process would have happened without the influence and grace of the various individuals and teachings I have come in contact with.

I was a graduate student in physics when my interest in and search for inner spiritual understanding began. I was studying physical science because I wanted to discover objective truth, truth independent from personal bias. By this time I was becoming convinced that the truth I was interested in was not what is explored by the physical sciences, but had more to do with the nature of being human.

I began with some experiential workshops focused on inner growth and openness, in the late sixties. This led me to undergoing a few years of bioenergetic analysis, with Michael Conant in Berkeley, which contributed a great deal to my opening up emotionally and physically. At the same time I began to study Sufi and Zen thought, reading mainly Idries Shah and D. T. Suzuki.

In 1971 I joined a group in Berkeley, where I was going to the University of California. The group was led by the Chilean Psychiatrist Claudio Naranjo. That group was the beginning of my direct contact with spiritual teaching, and the conscious launching of my inner journey. Dr. Naranjo, whom I related to as my teacher at the time, taught spiritual practice, mainly meditation, combined with psychological exploration. He combined his experience from Gestalt therapy and Karen Horney's self analysis with the map of the enneagram to teach the group to do in-depth psychological work. He lectured on many facets of spiritual development, and taught various meditations and spiritual exercises side by side with the intense psychological work. I credit him for teaching me that psychological work and spiritual practice can help each other and work together. I also learned from him various forms and structures for group and interpersonal work, some of which I later incorporated into my work with students. The work I did with Naranjo extended the emotional openness I had experienced with Conant to the spiritual dimension, bringing about my first experiences of Essence, chakra openings and some development of the three centers as taught by Gurdjieff. Dr. Naranjo used the Gurdjieffian concept of the contrast of Essence with personality. This notion had a great impact on the direction of my journey.

My few years of work with Dr. Naranjo provided many rich resources for my inner exploration, as he introduced his students to several excellent teachers from various ancient traditions. Through this connection I had the opportunity to work intensely for a couple of years with Tarthang Tulku Rinpoche. I learned from Rinpoche the basics of the Tibetan Buddhist view of reality, as well as numerous spiritual practices. Rinpoche taught Buddhist philosophy, especially regarding emptiness (sunyata) and Buddha nature, and Tibetan Buddhist psychology and its relation to spiritual practice and enlightenment. I also learned to practice vipassana meditation from Dhiravamsa, an ex-Theravada monk from Thailand. This association with Buddhist teaching and meditation led to various experiences of openness, spaciousness, emptiness and clarity.

At about that time I also had a brief contact with the enigmatic fourth-way teacher E. J. Gold. From Gold I learned about presence, simply by being in his presence. But the main thing I learned from him was about surrender. A short while later I began working with another fourth-way teacher, Henry Korman, an architect from New York. From Korman I learned an effective way of understanding and dealing with the superego, which we know mostly as the inner critic. I also learned from him the importance of practicing presence as self-remembering, and of taking care of everyday practical life. After Dr. Naranjo, he was the second major influence on my growing understanding that psychological work and spiritual practice can be combined effectively. He combined his Gurdjieffian-oriented spiritual practice with a Freudian-based approach to psychological experience. Around that time I also did a few years of work and training with a Reichian therapist, Dr. Philip Curcuruto, from whom I learned about Wilhelm Reich's work, and who helped me extend my physical and emotional openness to deeper and more refined levels of experience.

The work with these teachers and therapists helped me open to deeper aspects of myself, and I will always be grateful to them. I had many inner and spiritual experiences during this work, but they were disconnected and I did not have much understanding of them, nor of their relation to my usual experience. I view this period of working with various teachers as a stage that preceded the discoveries and transformation that became the source of my work, the Diamond Approach.

The transformation began with my discovery of Essence as presence, and my learning to stay anchored in this presence. This personal discovery of who and what I really am was a surprise, for it did not exactly correspond, as far as I knew, with the teachings I was familiar with. This recognition and realization of my essential nature as an ontological presence had volcanic effect on my life and my process. It became the center and meaning of my life from then on. This living presence began gradually to expand and deepen, revealing many aspects of Essence—qualities of presence like love, will, truth and so on—and various dimensions of Being. This process was a spontaneous unfoldment, what felt like a magical unveiling, a self-revelation of Being's mysteries.

This unfoldment disclosed not only many of the mysteries of Being, revealed as my nature and the nature of everything, but an amazing wealth of knowledge and understanding. The body of understanding that developed during my process is largely the product of the realization of a particular manifestation of Essence, which I came to recognize as essential guidance. This precise, diamond-like guidance became the inner guide that has functioned more truly than any external guide I have ever known. In fact the functioning of this guidance is so specific to the exact state, situation and understanding of the soul that no external guide could substitute for its realization and functioning as the guidance for an individual's spiritual awakening and development.

The understanding that developed was not merely an experiential comprehension of Essence in its various aspects and dimensions, but also a precise and detailed understanding of how these relate to the various manifestations of the ego self. I had learned that it was possible to do psychological work side by side with spiritual practice. In the course of my own transformation, I came upon a particular path in which the two are inseparable, and function as elements of the same method. It slowly dawned on me that what was happening was not only a personal transformation, but the development of a particular teaching that has a much wider applicability.

Inquiry into personal experience became the main method, in which psychological understanding opens the soul to deeper experiences, and also connects specific elements of the ego self—self-images, object relations, ego structures, identifications, personality patterns, emotional issues, etc.—with specific essential aspects and dimensions. The inquiry is mainly a matter of being aware of one's experience, both inner and outer, recognizing what is and what is not understood, and curiosity about it that expresses a heart-felt love for the truth. An important element in this inquiry is to be present with one's feelings and thoughts without expressing them or acting them out externally, thus opening the way to understanding them and their underlying dynamics.

The knowledge that developed has demonstrated such precision and universality that I have continuously been in awe of it. This awe led me to appreciate that this knowledge was not my personal creation, but the action of the guidance of Being. This knowledge became the basis of the Diamond Approach.

In other words, the Diamond Approach did not develop as a result of an intellectual synthesis of what I read, heard and experienced, but rather as an articulation of the terrain of an actual personal process of transformation. The synthesis is a discovery, not something created by an individual.

Shortly after my discovery of the nature of Essence, and its initial unfoldment, I shared my experience with two friends, who became important supports for both my personal unfoldment and the development of the Diamond Approach. When I discussed my experience with my friend Karen Johnson, who was living at the time in Colorado, she was able to perceive the essential presence in me, and this made it possible for her to begin experiencing it. As I shared my experience with my then old friend, Faisal Muqaddam, who had just come from Kuwait to California, he was also able to connect to and begin experiencing the essential presence. My exploration of Essence intensified and accelerated through the participation of these two friends. It helped a great deal that each of them already had a capacity for inner seeing, more developed than my own. My exploration expanded into intense collaboration and joint exploration with both Karen and Faisal. A couple of years later, when Karen moved to California, the three of us were able to explore the unfoldment together. We spent several years intensely exploring Essence and its development, both jointly and separately.

During these years I was introduced to psychoanalytic developmental psychology by Perry Segal, a friend who was doing his psychiatric residency in Denver. My attention was guided thus to the extensive study of the field of depth psychology, including Freud's work, ego psychology, self psychology, object relations theory, Reichian therapy and others. At the same time I studied the literature of several ancient traditions: Buddhism, Vedanta, Sufism, mystical Christianity, and others. I particularly benefited from the study of the works of, and sometimes contact with, teachers like G. I. Gurdjieff, Idries Shah, Ibn Arabi, Krishnamurti, Nisargadatta Maharaj, Ramana Maharshi, Aurobindo, Tarthang Tulku, Trungpa Rinpoche, the fourteenth Dalai Lama, and others. The exploration of these fields and teachings contributed to the development of the Diamond Approach, even though knowledge always arose from personal and direct experience of the perspectives and understandings of these teachers.

The applicability of the developing knowledge was amply confirmed not only by the perception and experience of Faisal and Karen, but mainly by the experiences and realizations of many of the students who worked with it. I began working with students in 1976, using the knowledge that was arising to guide the process of inner awakening in others. Some years later I began training teachers in the Diamond Approach. I have always been surprised by the power and efficacy of this emerging body of knowledge and the method accompanying it.

For close to twenty years now, Being has been continually revealing to me its many facets and dimensions, always in
spontaneous and unexpected revelations. This has transformed
my consciousness and life in ways I never dreamed of, and led
me to states of realization I never imagined existed. The collaboration with Faisal and Karen continued for about eight
years, until Faisal decided to go his own way, about nine years
ago, for personal reasons and because he felt it important to be
on his own. I will always be grateful and indebted to him for his
part in my personal unfoldment and his contribution to the
development of the Diamond Approach. Karen and I continue
the intense joint exploration, which has taken the unfoldment
to ever more subtle dimensions and realms, and to a deepening and clarifying of both the perspective and the method. My
indebtedness to Karen is not only for her deep friendship, her
contribution to my personal unfoldment and the development
of the Diamond Approach, but also for shouldering the difficult
responsibility of helping me develop and run the Ridhwan
school. Our friendship, rooted as it is in the exploration of the
truth of Being, has traversed depths and domains unknown in
most friendships.

I would like also to express my gratitude to my long-time
friend Ronald Kane, for the supportive deep friendship and for
the many discussions and exchanges of views and experience
relating to both inner experience of Being and work with students. My gratitude also goes to Larry Spiro, Ph.D., who quickly
became a friend after I did some classes and workshops for him
as part of the Melia Institute. We engaged in many discussions
of the logoi of East and West, and he introduced me to the teachings of Dzogchen and Kashmir Shaivism. Coming into contact
with these nondual teachings helped me to clarify some of the
subtle questions that have emerged in my continuing unfoldment and transformation. This has helped my understanding of
the Diamond Approach become sharper and more complete.

Towards the second part of the spontaneously unfolding revelation of Being, my process became focused not on the

experience of Being and its essential manifestations, but on the shift of identity to Being. This led to the development of self-recognition in increasingly subtler and more profound dimensions of Being, culminating in the realization of the absolute. This then ushered me into the subtle process of the clarification of the soul to the degree necessary for it to be a personal vehicle for the absolute nature, setting the ground for further revelations of unexpected dimensions of experience. After the first few chapters, which set the stage for this process, it is this thread of experience that *Luminous Night's Journey* addresses. It must be mentioned that this process occurred at the time within a larger process of unfoldment, discovery and understanding. This book focuses on only a small part of the overall process, tracing the particular thread of integrating the soul into the absolute. This subtle process occurred as a thread that lasted for a few years, but my overall process of unfolding continued beyond this subprocess, and still continues.

This book, and all my previous publications, owe a great deal to the various editors who prepared them for publication. My debt to my chief editor, Alia Johnson, is inestimable, for without her and her great dedication, energy and intelligence my work would not have been available to interested readers in such excellent form and quality. I am also indebted to Morton Letofsky for the energy and care he contributed toward the development and structuring of the Ridhwan school and its various organizations. My gratitude also goes to my wife, Marie, and to many of the students and teachers in the Ridhwan School, whose dedication and effort have been a great support for the development of the school and the publication of the books. Many have contributed to making this work available to a widening circle of individuals looking for a fresh outlook on spiritual experience and integration.

A.H. Almaas
January, 1994
Kona, Hawaii

Luminous Night's Journey

The trees are silent,
The mountain is still, and
The man is gone.

One

Intimacy

Late afternoon, just back from my office, after a full day of eventful teaching sessions with students. I lie down in bed, mildly tired. I can feel the psychic layers that I have taken on from students peeling off, one by one. As each layer peels away, it reveals its content—emotions, thoughts, images, physical tensions. This process leaves me clearer and lighter. The lightness opens further, revealing spaciousness. Consciousness manifests as empty, transparent space, light and clean.

In this spaciousness my own thoughts and feelings appear: a constellation of thoughts and subtle feelings, all related to images and impressions about my identity, about who I am. This psychic cluster, like a cloud in the spaciousness of mind, provides the mind with the familiar feeling of identity, an identity totally dependent on memories of my past experience. Contemplating the totality of the cluster, without taking an inner position about it, I recognize that it is a mental phenomenon. On seeing this, I become distinctly aware that it is external to me. The feeling-recognition is: "this is not me."

The focus of attention spontaneously shifts. The psychic cluster gently fades away, almost imperceptibly, like a cloud slowly dissipating. When it is gone, what is left is simplicity, a clear and simple sense of presence without self-reflection. There are no thoughts about the experience, no feelings about it, only the simplicity of presence. Clarity, space, stillness and lucidity bring a sense of a crisp cloudless sky around a snow-capped mountain top.

The sun is about to set, and the windows open on the East, so the bedroom is somewhat dark. The sun illuminates some of the hillside, while the rest is steadily cooled by the expanding gentle shade. The flowers in the pots outside the room appear bright; the green leaves glisten. Lucidity pervades everything: the flower pots, the trees, the distant clouds, the deep blue sky. All is pristine, undisturbed by wind or thought.

Green grass,
Lemons on the tree,
The vast blue sky.

In the lucidity of space, a question appears, carefree and delighted: "And what is me?" Nothing recognizable by memory. I experience myself, without a feeling of self, as the simplicity of presence, which is now a simplicity of perception, a bare witnessing. There is no inner dialogue, and no commentary on what is perceived. The perceiving is without a perceiver, awareness without an observer. Without self-reflection, the simplicity of presence is merely the simplicity of witnessing. I am a witness of all in the field of vision, a witness with no inside. The witness is merely the witnessing. The only thing left from familiar experience is the location of witnessing, which seems to be determined by the location of the body. The body is relaxed and clear. The sense of the body is more of luminosity than of sensation, witnessed as part of the environment.

Time does not seem to pass; it has come to a stop. When the psychic constellation that has given me the familiar sense of identifying myself ceases, the sense of the passage of time is gone. In the simplicity of presence, time does not pass, for the sense of the passage of time is simply the continuity of the feeling of the familiar identity.

Simplicity of presence, when it is complete, is timelessness. Timelessness is completely being the simplicity of presence. Timelessness is not an idea, a thought in the mind. It is the fullness of the experience of presence of Being, pure and prior to thought or self-reflection.

A few days later...

Upon waking up in the morning, I find my attention riveted by a feeling of hurt in the heart. The hurt is warm and sad. It feels like the heart is wounded in its very flesh. The hurt leads to a gnawing sensation in the mobius, the subtle center at the sternum. The gnawing is painful; it feels physically grating, but also emotionally difficult. A frustrated feeling has become stuck at the lower part of the chest, turning into a gnawing sensation. I feel all this mixed with the feeling of hurt and sadness.

I contemplate the hurt, the sadness and the physical contraction. Holding all in awareness, while intimately feeling all of the nuances of the ongoing experience. The contemplating awareness embraces the content of experience with a feeling of warm kindness and with an attitude of curiosity, not knowing what the hurt is about, but interested to find out. The gnawing sensation responds to the motiveless inquiry, and begins to soften as the contraction at the mobius center relaxes, revealing an unexpected element to the sadness: loneliness. The hurt turns out to be the pain of feeling lonely. The feeling of loneliness wets the sadness with more tears, and the hurt expands into an emptiness underlying the sadness. Now it is deep, sad loneliness.

But why, why am I feeling lonely?

There does not seem to be any reason for it. I am still in bed, my wife, Marie, lying asleep beside me. I feel my affection for her, but this does not touch the sad loneliness. The loneliness continues even though I am not alone.

I get up, go to the bathroom to wash, the loneliness following me, filling the space of the bathroom with its teary sadness. The question continues to live, while I shave: what is making me feel lonely? Here, memory reminds me of the experience of the last few days, that of the simplicity of presence and witnessing. Reflecting on it, I intuit that there is a connection between the experience of simple presence and the feeling of loneliness. My curiosity intensifies, a throbbing sensation at the forehead begins to luminate.

The throbbing lumination at the forehead reveals itself to be a diamond-clear and colorful presence. The more passionate the naturally curious contemplation is about the loneliness, the more alive and brilliant becomes this presence, manifesting spacious and discerning clarity. I recognize the variegated, scintillating presence as the discriminating intelligence, the true *nous*, which appears as a presencing of the intensification of consciousness, at the center of the forehead, to reveal the meaning of experience. The intensification of inquiry coincides with a greater and more definite presence of the discriminating intelligence, revealing its exquisite sense of delicate precision.

The experience now is a field of sadness, loneliness and emptiness, combined with the memory of the simplicity of presence, all opening up to the scintillatingly alive presence of the *nous*. Insights begin to radiate out from the scintillating consciousness. Perceptually, the operation of the *nous* appears as a multicolored glittering radiance; affectively, it is a delicate and pleasant expansive clarity; cognitively, it is the spontaneous arising of insight.

The understanding unfolds: the sense of simplicity in the experience of presence is finding myself as the presence of Being, totally and purely, without thoughts or feelings about it. There is simplicity because there remains only the purity of presence, with no memory and no mind. This absence of mind, in the completeness of being presence, is tantamount to the absence of everything that mind carries. During the experience of the last few days I saw how the mind creates and carries the sense of familiar identity of the self, which it accomplishes through memory and self-reflection. What I did not see then, but was implicit in the experience, is that the mind carries also the sense of the other—of another person—again by using memory.

Here, I remember the insight of the object relation psychologists: the sense of self develops in conjunction with the sense of other, first the mother then all others. The understanding is that the familiar sense of identity develops from *early on within a field of object relations, always in relation to another person. This sense of self becomes a felt continuity by the memories of these experiences of oneself coalescing into a fixed structure in the psyche. Hence, this psychic structure also contains the memories of interactions with significant others.**

When I felt the sense of familiar identity disappear I did not see that this also meant the disappearance of all impressions of others. In other words, as the activity of the mind comes to a stop, all the feelings dependent on the internalized memories disappear. This understanding shows me that the sense of familiar identity always includes, explicitly or implicitly, the feeling of others. The feeling of self swims in an atmosphere of internalized relationships.

This normally ever-present atmosphere of an interpersonal world ceases in the experience of the simplicity of presence, allowing presence to be alone. This aloneness of presence is its simplicity. Recently I have been experiencing it as simplicity, but this experience shows me that I have unconsciously reacted to it as total aloneness.

Here, the feeling of emptiness deepens into a dark abyss, and the loneliness disappears into a singular state of aloneness, existential and fundamental. A hint of sadness remains, in the form of a subtle, warm feeling pervading the deepening emptiness. The throbbing presence at the forehead again scintillates brightly; this time emerald green outshines its other living colors. The sadness reveals associations with the state of aloneness: times in childhood when I was left alone. In the emptiness of the mind float memories of a sad and lonely child, left alone, sometimes forgotten.

---

* The sections in italics throughout the book are additions written at the time of putting my journal into book form. They are not part of the original journal, but are added to create needed context, and to fill in the gaps in the narrative.

Recognizing that the source of the feeling of loneliness is my association of the painful loneliness of the past with the state of aloneness of presence in the present, liberates the sadness, allowing it to evaporate, leaving a sense of transparent depth to the dark abyss, a spacious depth. The feeling is centered in the chest, as if the chest region has become void of everything, except for a subtle lightness which curiously feels deep. Feeling within the chest, inquiring with no goal in mind, I find no sense of solidity. The chest feels empty, but curiously quiet, peaceful and still. I recognize the state as a luminous black spaciousness, which is the unity of stillness and space. There is immaculate, glistening emptiness, but the emptiness has a sense of depth. The depth seems to be the felt aspect of the blackness of space. It is like looking into, and feeling into, starless deep space.

The depth, although void, has a soft texture, an exquisite gentleness. There is a sense of comfort, safety and a carefree trust, as if the vastness of intergalactic space has mysteriously evolved into a gentle and loving medium. It is not a cold space, not an impersonal space, but a space that feels exactly like what the human soul has perennially longed for: the warmth of mother's breasts, the softness of delicate velvet, a quiet shining blissfulness and an endless generosity.

My chest has become an opening into an infinitely deep and dark space, which feels clear and void of all extraneous things. Also, inseparable from the transparent voidness, is the presence of love itself. Now I can taste the pleasurable sweetness of love on my tongue, and throughout the whole chest cavity.

As I proceed to the dining room, I feel myself inseparable from the total stillness of this loving space. The mind is quiet and peaceful, the body relaxed and its movements easy. As I begin breakfast with Marie, the sweet quietness envelopes us. We talk about the practical things of the day, but now I begin to recognize another dimension to the loving void.

At the beginning this seems to be related to our easy and simple conversation, where the peaceful sweetness divulges itself as a delicate contact between us, a subtle intimacy. I like the gentle intimacy, and awareness gently focuses on its exquisite sensation. There are lightness and depth, spaciousness and softness, clarity and sweetness. The feeling of intimacy is not new in my experience. However, I slowly realize that I feel intimate not only with Marie, but also with the food, with the table cloth, with the chairs, even with the walls. I feel intimate with everything I am aware of, in an atmosphere of gentle quiet and relaxed openness. Everything seems to have now this quality of softness and contactfulness. More accurately, everything seems to be bathed in this intimate spaciousness, as if everything is sharing itself, with total generosity and complete openness.

Intimacy discloses itself as an inherent quality of this black inner space. The intimacy is not only a matter of me being intimate with another person, or with the environment. It is not a matter of a subject intimately relating to an object. The chest cavity is pervaded by the essence of intimacy, a black spaciousness inseparable from delicate lovingness.

At this point the jewel-like *nous* at the forehead manifests mostly black radiance, coextensive with the sensation of delicately faceted, satin, liquid energy.

The more I recognize that intimacy is a quality of spacious consciousness, the more distinctly I know it: velvet-fine openness, deep spaciousness, delicate softness, sweet stillness. The chest has become an entrance into an exquisitely heartful night sky. All of this distills itself into something unique and utterly human: intimacy. It is as if the space is a refined consciousness intimately in contact with its very nature at each point of its spaciousness. And this total openness and contact becomes an intimacy with everything, totally independent of mind and memory.

No loneliness and no sense of aloneness. Simplicity of Being has ushered me, through the door of aloneness, into its inherent intimacy.

It is not that the fist needs to open up.
It is not a matter of surrender,
There is no fist to start with.

Two

The Personal Trap

For some time I have been noticing an unexpected and strange sort of perception. At the beginning, it is difficult to focus on this awareness, for it comes in subtle intimations, fleeting intuitions, of a form of experience with which I am unfamiliar. It appears that inexhaustible Being is divulging a new manifestation, but so far in flashes and feelings, rather than in a full and clear manifestation. One such feeling is the intuition that there exists an awareness which is constant, always present, but not involved with whatever is happening. As the feeling becomes stronger the intuition becomes more specific: there exists the life process, with a person or a personal consciousness involved with it, or as part of it, but there exists also and concomitantly another kind of consciousness. This constant background consciousness is always aware of what is happening in the life process without being involved in it, even though the personal consciousness is sometimes so involved in what is happening that it becomes lost in it.

I intuit the existence of a consciousness that forms a constant background for the everyday personal consciousness, but is separate from and transcends it. Once in a while, as the intuition becomes strong and explicit, I become directly aware of this background consciousness, which I recognize as the source of the intuitions and intimations.

This consciousness, new in my experience, arises and meets the ordinary personal consciousness, and this meeting appears in the mind as flashes of intuition. As these intimations become clearer, the new clarity makes it possible for awareness to perceive more openly, accurately and directly the new sense of consciousness, which becomes now a direct perception. The experience still occurs in fleeting flashes, but these become strong enough to expose the sectors of the ordinary consciousness which function as obstacles to clearer awareness of the background consciousness.

Today, what is exposed by the impact of the arising consciousness is an awareness of how thoroughly I am lost in my personal life. I have the strong impression of being imprisoned by all the elements of my life, whether I like it or not. I become aware of how involved I am in my life: in my relationships, work, interests, writing, reading, books, house, family, students, ideas and thoughts, preferences and prejudices, everything that forms the content of my life. The absorption in my life situations, whether I experience it as desirable or not, is much more ubiquitous and thoroughgoing than I have imagined. This is true even with respect to the parts of my life that I feel are free and expanded, rewarding and fulfilling. Even deep experiences of realization of Being, of understanding fundamental truths and perceiving new dimensions, ensnare me. I become part of the experience, inseparable from it, and limited by it. I am seeing that because of the lack of a comparative frame of reference, involvement in my life imperceptibly becomes enmeshment.

The perception deepens into the understanding that not only am I enmeshed, some important aspect of me is actually lost in this involvement in my life. Understanding bequeaths its offspring: the action of Being in the direction of optimizing its presentations, here activating Being in its tendency to maximize personal experience. As usual, understanding opens consciousness to deeper and more expanded levels of Being. Experientially, understanding manifests at this point as the intensification of the glittering throbbing at the center of the forehead, while the action of Being manifests as the unfoldment of conscious experience into new presentations. This arises now as a feeling, unbidden, of wanting to be free from all this personal life. I am aware of intuiting myself to be beyond all personal life, and of wanting this truth to come to some experiential fruition.

Although I am aware of wanting something beyond this experience, I do not reject the perception of the experience of the personal life; thus the experience shifts from awareness of wanting more to a clearer perception of what is actually here in my experience. I can feel the totality of this life, my life: its present, past and future. It feels distinct and separate from who I am. The throbbing at the forehead develops into a sense of expanded clarity: I realize that there is usually the tendency to use all this content of the experience of my life to define me. This content limits not only what I experience, but also, and most importantly, the experience of who and what I am. This is particularly obvious in the case of thoughts, for I see that I can think only along certain lines. Although I might have many new thoughts and ideas, the general mental atmosphere remains the same. I see that the mind flows in predetermined grooves, where change is only a matter of the widening or narrowing of these grooves.

I feel that this is not right. There is a sense that I am beyond all of this. I feel, with some kind of inexplicable certainty, that any content of experience cannot contain or define me. Even fundamental functions I perform in my life, like being a father or a teacher, are just roles I have adopted, and they must not and cannot define or contain me. I am quite beyond all of it. I deeply feel a longing not to be caught by the content of my personal life. This feeling comes from an unknown place, where the concern is not with a particular emotion or state, but with the totality of the personal life. I do not feel any value judgment regarding my personal life, whether it is good or not, whether it is happy and fulfilled or not, whether it is desirable or not. There is only the longing to go beyond it, because of the felt certainty that I am in fact beyond it. This longing is for the truth to manifest, the truth which I am beginning to glimpse.

At this point, I cannot discern clearly what I am that is beyond my personal life and its content. Yet there is some kind of emptiness or awareness, with the feeling that I am something beyond all of what I have experienced in the totality of my life, and that I have adopted roles only in order to do certain things.

A few days later...

These intimations, feelings and intuitions continue for a few days, clarifying sometimes into fleeting glimpses of a background awareness. This has been allowing a greater capacity to see and understand personal situations and the feelings around them, engendering a state of personal happiness and contentment.

One of these days, in the afternoon, I begin to experience a dense heaviness near the stomach. The stomach area comes to feel thick, dense, bulky and heavy. I observe that the sensation of heaviness in this particular location makes it difficult for me to do my work, for I need to be empty and open to have the sensitivity that my work requires. I remember now feeling the same sensation the night before, when I felt as if someone had punched me in the stomach. The awareness now, as I contemplate the experience, is that there is something like a big slug in the area of the stomach. It gradually becomes clear, as I continue to be present to it, that it is a presence of some manifestation of consciousness which feels lead-like. There is a sensation of something that feels almost like an object, which is heavy, opaque and dense, but also with the somewhat soft, thick and metallic texture of lead.

For a long time my inner experience has included a dimension that can best be described as alchemical. "Alchemical" describes the sense of my own presence as different substantial qualities which transform. It began when I first discovered that I could experience presence instead of only feelings and thoughts. I saw also that I could experience this presence as the substantial existence of various inner forms. The presence sometimes takes the form of naturally occurring substances, like lead, iron, gold, mercury, wood, water, air, clouds, bone, diamonds, pearls, and so on. The experience is not exactly the same as seeing or touching these naturally occurring manifestations, but of qualities of consciousness that take forms that feel or look like these phenomena. I experience inner sensations of texture and temperature, taste, sight and sound, which correspond exactly to the naturally manifesting substances, although it is clear that they are manifestations of consciousness. This kind of experience is unusual in our everyday awareness, but this realm of experience becomes available at a certain depth of spiritual development, and in time becomes a normal part of ongoing experience. This dimension of perception greatly enriches our understanding, and endows it with a definiteness and precision not available in normal experience, for each form expresses a specific meaning. Some of these forms are the basis of metaphors in various languages. For example, when we feel "crystal clear" it is possible to perceive that this is the effect of an arising presence in the form of a faceted diamond in the head. These meanings can be known precisely only through the operation of the diamond-like nous.

By night I realize the thickness is a lead ball, what I would call a lead pearl. However, as I remain aware of it, it begins to attain a diamond-like hardness that lead does not usually possess, as if the leaden ball at the stomach has become faceted and crystallized. In other words, the heaviness has become quite specific, taking the form of what could be called a diamond lead pearl.

The feeling in this faceted leaden hardness is similar to the essential quality of will, but has also a sense of existence. Will, as a specific aspect of Being, feels like a solidity with the felt characteristics of immovability, determination and persistence, almost like a natural and healthy stubbornness. Will is a quality I recognize, which makes it possible to understand the meaning of the present experience of the diamond lead pearl. The throbbing sensation at the forehead, indicating the presence of *nous*, begins to luminate, a lumination that translates into precise understanding of what I am experiencing. I recognize the faceted leaden heaviness as an imitation of an essential manifestation of Being, the true will to exist.

The awareness of the phenomenon of an imitative quality reflects the understanding that the ego cannot be original. Whatever quality it develops is bound to be a reflection of an essential quality. Its strength reflects essential strength, its intelligence essential intelligence, and so on. These reflections can be seen as imitations, when we know the essential qualities. They are similar to the essential qualities in some ways, but lack the aliveness and luminosity of the real ones.

This recognition clarifies the significance of a passing feeling that I have had in the past few days, that there is something in my experience of myself that never changes. I did not know at the time how true this feeling was, and whether it had any significance, partly because the inquiry has been focused on a different line of investigation, the trap of involvement in the content of personal life. Now I see that my concern with the limitations inherent in the involvement in the content of the personal life was a first glimpse of this thread of experience. As the *nous* radiates more intensely, I begin to realize that I am perceiving another facet of the situation of being trapped in the particulars of personal life.

The realization dawns on me now that in spite of all the deep knowledge, understanding and realization I have attained so far, which has radically transformed my experience, there is something in me that never changes, is never affected by these realizations, something in me that never moves. I recognize the leaden heaviness as an imitation of the will to exist, along with awareness of something that does not change in relation to the involvement in personal life. The *nous* synthesizes these observations into the unexpected insight that it is the totality of the personality which does not change. So it is not a *part* of the ego-self that does not change, but the totality of this self, the familiar self.

Until now, my investigation has involved exploring various sectors of the personality, as part of the realization of particular qualities of Being. My inquiry now involves awareness of the totality of the self underlying this experience. *Nous* illuminates the situation by revealing that what has not changed so far is the totality of the personality. I continue to be the same person, with the same characteristics and preferences, even though there has been an amazing expansion of experience, to include many new dimensions of Being.

This insight naturally unfolds into the question of what is responsible for this lack of transformation. This question is heralded by the brightening of the yellow facet of the radiant *nous*. If sectors of the personality have transformed under the impact of the realization of aspects of Being, why does not this change the whole?

Now, understanding the leaden pearl, I begin to see what is responsible for the unchangeability of the personality as a whole. What I have not seen or investigated so far is what supports this totality. A quality or dimension which provides a ground for any segment can be perceived as the support for that segment. But I have never even suspected that the personality, as a whole, possesses its own support. The recognition arrives in a flash of exhilarating insight: it is the leaden heaviness which functions as this support, manifesting as the will to exist as the separate individual of ego.

> *The* nous *has the capacity to integrate elements of knowledge, from past understanding and present experience, in all known dimensions of experience, and synthesize the various elements into an insight that illuminates what I am investigating at the moment. This is not a thinking process, although logical thinking is one facet of it. It is the functioning of discriminating intelligence using all capacities of knowing and understanding inherent to consciousness, simultaneously as one act.*
>
> *I can see in retrospect some of the elements synthesized by the* nous *in arriving at the overarching insight about the*

support for the totality of the personality. This analysis is also the functioning of the nous, for my personal mind could not have this global analysis and understanding:

    i.   *Lead indicates inertia, unchanging manifestation, conditioned inflexible existence.*

   ii. *Hence, lead functions as the support for all conditioned patterns. Any pattern in the self will continue to exist, even after it is fully investigated and understood, until an inertia implicit in it is seen and understood. This inertia usually reveals itself to be the expression of the presence of leaden consciousness underlying the particular pattern. More specifically, the leaden heaviness is the substantial alchemical form that inertia takes in consciousness. When this lead quality is recognized the inertia supporting the particular pattern is seen.*

  iii. *In the language of substantial or alchemical forms of consciousness, the pearl signifies personalness of experience. The pearl form appears both on the ego and essential dimensions of experience, always indicating a personal manifestation. Specifically, the pearl as a form of consciousness indicates the presence of the total individuality, the presence of the person in his wholeness, whether on the ego level or the essential level of Being. The pearl appears as a sphere of compact consciousness that possesses a pearly sheen.*

  iv. *The facetedness of any form of consciousness signifies objective understanding or knowledge of what it is. In other words, when any quality of consciousness, like gold for instance, appears in a faceted jewel-like form, it indicates an objective understanding of what this form, gold, is.*

   v. *Existence is an essential aspect of Being. Being reveals itself to be the true existence of any manifestation. However, when Being reveals itself as the experience of true existence it manifests in a specific form, an immense presence of unusual density, solidity and reality. This form of presence has the shiny gray color of the metal molybdenum, but the mass and density of hematite.*

vi. *The aspect of existence functions partly as a form of will. It can be experienced as the will to exist. Here there is a doorway to other dimensions of essential experience, where each essential aspect can manifest in deeper and deeper dimensions of objectivity. In one of these dimensions each of the aspects functions as a form of will.*

vii. *The personality does not have true or essential existence, but conditioned existence. This conditioned existence, which appears as the unchanging manifestation of its patterns, depends on the inflexibility, rigidity, and fixation of these patterns. This inertia supports its continued appearance, which we ordinarily perceive as its existence. Therefore, inertia is what gives the personality patterns and sectors their apparent existence. In other words, the lead quality of consciousness is responsible for the continued existence of manifestations of the personality. This is the reason I understand the inner experience of lead to be an indication of false or apparent existence. Inertia is the support that is responsible for the unchangeability of a manifestation of personality. Being aware of this inertia as lead in one's experience is to experience this phenomenon in the realm of alchemical forms.*

The presence of lead points to the inertia supporting a manifestation of personality. The form of lead as a pearl points to the fact that this support is for the totality of the personality, which is the sense of being an individual, a separate person. The hard facetedness of the leaden ball means this is the objective understanding of the support for the totality of the personality. Since lead indicates false existence, and existence functions as will, then the diamond lead pearl means the objective understanding of the will of the ego to exist as a total individuality, a separate person.

> *The insight does not arise as the end result of such log-*
> *ical analysis. The existence and operation of the nous is a*
> *nonlocal phenomenon. The nous synthesizes beyond time;*
> *I can perceive only some of its functioning, and only when*
> *I am interested in the process of the arising of insight itself.*
> *Otherwise, I experience only the flash of insight, which is*
> *the cognitive aspect of the glittering radiance of the nous'*
> *presence.*
>
> *At this point in my process the nous synthesizes all*
> *these elements, all previous insights by nous, into the over-*
> *arching new insight: the support for the totality of the per-*
> *sonality is the will to exist as an ego.*

This clarifies many previous experiences, like the heaviness that appears near the stomach when I feel that someone
is blunting my personal expression. I recognize now that at such
times the lead pearl surfaces close to consciousness, because I
must experience such thwarting of personal expression as a
threat to my personal existence.

Insight expands now to synthesize the understanding of
being trapped in my personal life, and the recognition of the presence of inertia responsible for the unchangeability of the totality of the personality. This lead pearl is the determination/will
of the personal existence of the ego, which has been unconscious till now, although implicit in all ego manifestations. As long
as I am under the sway of this will of inertia, I will be enmeshed
in my personal life whenever I am involved with any experience.
In other words, the personal life continues to be the life of the
totality of the personality, the life of the separate person of ego.
This unconscious identification will always subsume new experiences and insights into its own personal life, turning them into
possessions of the person of ego. My sense of myself has been
trapped in my personal life because I have always had, unrec-
ognized, the will to exist as the familiar individual.

The deepening insight into my personal experience and
the personal inertia that underlies it, allows the leaden heaviness

to gradually expand and dominate the consciousness. I am now this faceted, hard and spherical leaden density, immovable and unchangeable. This is curious. There is the feeling of expansion that accompanies the flow of insights, but there is also the thickening of consciousness as it becomes dominated by the leaden heaviness. However, there is no resistance to the leaden, thick consciousness which functions as the ground of the ego experience of self, and no value judgment about it. There is merely the openness to what is arising, and the curiosity that manifests as an open and open-ended inquiry into it. This openness and curiosity creates the space necessary for the arising and operation of the *nous*.

A kind of happy love appears at the left side of the body, a golden love with a sense of purity that gives it a sense of being divine. This love, sweet and light, quickens the consciousness, acting as the active agent, alchemically transforming its qualities. The heaviness of lead persists, side by side with lightness, openness and joy.

To slough off the universe
To be utterly naked
God is alone.

Three

The Impersonal

A few days later...

I wake up in the morning with a slight tension at the left shoulder. There is discomfort with the tension. Simply being aware of the tension seems to influence it by making it expand. It becomes a line of tension along the left side of the chest, enfolded by a soft cushiony sensation.

> *This line is a manifestation of the ego-self that I call the "ego-line." It usually accompanies a specific psychic contraction that corresponds to the presence of the individuality of ego. In other words, the ego-line is the physical manifestation of the ego structure that gives the personality or ego-self the sense of being a separate individual, an autonomous person. The line of tension is a direct indication that the sense of being an individual on the ego level is a contraction of consciousness. This separate individuality of ego is formed or defined mostly by the separating boundaries, both bodily and psychological.*

The soft cushiony sensation around the line of tension turns out to be a manifestation of consciousness that relates to a false sense of being a person. This makes sense, for the ego-line represents the person of ego, which is not an essential form, but imitates the essential form of the personal essence. As I recognize its falseness, it begins slowly to flake off, falling off the line of tension like dead skin falling off a mummy. This process goes on for most of the day.

Later in the day, the line of tension becomes a tube of a plastic-like substance, an empty plastic tube, which extends all the way to the top of the head. As I go about the business of the day, I do not lose touch with this contraction, but remain continuously aware of it as part of my conscious experience. At some point, this contemplation opens the way for a very subtle insight: my concern about the contraction is inseparable from the contraction. The concern involves a desire for the contraction not to be there, which I now recognize as my hope to go beyond it. The plastic tube contraction is the presence of the individual of ego in the posture of hoping to go beyond itself. The hope is inseparable from the contraction, because it is the future-oriented attitude of the personality, which is the contraction. As I see this, the contraction begins to dissolve. The tube of contraction first dissolves in the head, which eliminates the mental concern. A beautiful sky blue quality of consciousness appears in the head, bringing a sense of mental rest and relaxation. Poignant settledness of all agitation in the head. The head feels filled by a delicious sensation that seems to smoothly dissolve any form in this part of the body.

As this happens, and as the totality of the tube of contraction disappears, I lose the sense of being a person, and become an awareness that recedes indefinitely, as if backward, from the familiar sense of being a person, until I recognize myself as a new kind of witnessing. I become an immaterial witness, not located within a personal consciousness. I find myself to be a witnessing of all phenomena.

A new obstacle arises at this point, a belief that constitutes a resistance against this new manifestation. This belief interferes with the sense of witnessing, without totally eliminating it. The belief is that there will be no personal life, no personal living, if there is no enmeshment in life. This exposes the belief as part of the inertia of being the separate individual of ego.

Being responds to this concern by manifesting the aspect of the personal essence, the pearl beyond price, the person of Being. The experience transforms into knowing myself as a full presence, rounded as a pearl, but transparent and sweet. I feel personal, even though I am a pure presence of transparent consciousness. This transparent fullness has a subtle sweetness, making it feel slightly sticky, or gummy. There is pure presence, with clarity and spaciousness all around. The cognitive aspect of the experience is that I am a person with no qualities, only a personal presence, devoid of images or psychological boundaries. Since I can be a person without being the product of memory, I can live a personal life without getting lost in it.

That night, during dinner, the leaden heaviness appears again, scattering the attention and presence for about an hour. The leaden heaviness becomes so dense that it disintegrates most of my capacity for attention and presence. Strong resistances arise, feelings of rubbery thickness, wooden dryness, amorphous states of consciousness, and many other confused and chaotic sensations. I feel the leaden rounded heaviness pushing from inside, scattering whatever consciousness it meets in its way. At this point I realize that the power of this heaviness arises from the transformation of the leaden consciousness into something much more substantial and powerful. The lead pearl has transformed into the shiny gray existence pearl, like a large pearl of hematite.

I feel personal but immense, a person of Being so dense that my substantiality eclipses the physical substantiality of the body. The most definite feeling is a sense of personal existence. I feel intensely real, existing so fundamentally that the mind cannot conceive of this reality. I experience myself as a person, and this person is composed of pure existence. Existence of Being, essential and fundamental, and independent of the mind, forms the very atoms of what I am. I am existence, beyond all thought of existence. The sense of truth and reality is immensely profound; it feels deeper than the universe itself. And this unimaginably real sense of existence has a very subtle sense of being a person—a person not defined by history or mind, not confined by character traits or relationships, but a person who exists, and that is all. The sense of existence has an unquestionable sense of certainty, independent of any content of mind or experience. I recognize at this point that there is no basis for the concern that there will be no personal life if I am not enmeshed in it.

This experience of being so real and certain as a person continues throughout dinner. I continue to converse with my dinner companions, while I am spontaneously attending to the inner transformation. The unusually substantial sense of presence affects the atmosphere at dinner in a subtle way not recognized by my companions. The conversation merely turns towards basic things in life, less abstract and more personal. My body feels as if all of its atoms are pulled downward, as if gravity has increased, but there is no physical discomfort. In fact, the body relaxes; the muscles let go and condense downward.

I realize that there is no real basis for believing that in order to have a personal life I need to be enmeshed in it. This is true for the person of ego, who is formed by images and psychological patterns. Now, however, I have the certainty that my personal existence is beyond any of that. My personal existence is beyond mind and history, for it is an essential manifestation of the fundamental existence of Being. I can be a person, and live a personal life in a truly involved way, without being enmeshed in any of its particulars. This is certain.

> *I have experienced my presence in the essential form of the pearl innumerable times. This essential form manifests mostly as a luminous white pearl, but can manifest in the color of any essential aspect, like the deep sky blue of direct knowing, the emerald green of loving kindness, or the shiny gold of truth. In each of these manifestations, the particular aspect, with all its alchemical characteristics, is experienced along with the characteristic of personalness. The presence of the pearl signifies authentic personalness, which reveals the possibility of living a personal life from the view of Being.*
>
> *The existence pearl is the new development of the personal aspect of Being. It is quite amazing to see how Being resolves a particular issue, or answers a real question, not*

by an insight or idea, but by the presentation of an essential form of its own truth. The resolution is an experience of Being, in one of its pure and universal forms, and not merely the dissolution of an obstacle or the end of a conflict. The beautiful thing about such a resolution is how exact and precise it is. Being responds with the precise state needed for the resolution, a state not anticipated by the mind, arising as an unexpected discovery. Such experiences demonstrate the awesome intelligence that Being possesses, which can only fill us with awe, and heart-felt gratitude and trust.

The concern that I started with involved the belief that there would be no personal life if there were no enmeshment in it. I believed I would not exist as a person if I were not enmeshed in the particulars of my life. Being revealed, through its messenger, the nous, *that my personal existence is an essential manifestation of Being, independent of mind and situations, and hence stands on its own, independent of mental reactions. In other words, I can live a personal life by merely being, for my personal existence is a part of Being. There is no real threat to my personal existence. Before this point, I had not experienced existence of Being, itself, as a personal presence. The response of Being to my concern is exquisitely precise, beyond all expectations.*

By the time dinner is over, the density and substantiality suddenly evaporate, revealing a vastness beyond comprehension. I do not perceive this vastness, but I recognize it as my very identity. I experience myself as the vast silent dark emptiness. As I experience this new identity, I learn a great deal of what I truly am when I am not trapped in the particulars of personal life and history. I can be present as personal existence, or I can transcend all personal experience. I am then the unchanging background witnessing, which has been revealing itself in the midst of personal experience, in glimpses and intimations, flashes and intuitions. Now this awareness reveals itself fully, as the universal witness.

I experience myself as beyond everything, literally everything, and not just everything in my personal life. I am a silent witness, vast and unchanging, beyond time and all space. I am absolutely still, totally uninvolved, but completely aware. This demonstrates directly that I do not need to be freed or enlightened. I am always free, always have been and always will be. Also, I cannot be trapped, for my very identity is totally detached awareness. I can see my personal life as a drama that I do not have to be involved in. It is like a movie that has a beginning and an end, but it is not me. I feel distant from everything, but acutely aware of everything.

I am a silent space, totally empty but containing everything. The recognition, which is a direct perception, is that everything is in me. The body, the universe, essence, personality, everything that can become an object of perception, is not me, but is in me. I am pure awareness, mere witnessing, where everything arises and passes away.

Four days later...

I wake up with the black space of intimacy, feeling pervaded by and enfolded in a sweet deliciousness. At the center of this deep intimacy, I sense the solid and dense presence of a diamond-like inner support. This brings a sense of grounded solid reality. At the same time there is spaciousness and depth. The body-mind is functioning mostly as a location for the consciousness. The spacious depth continues during the day, expanding gradually into the vastness of the silent witness. The experience of the universal witness unfolds more than it did few days ago, revealing further implications of recognizing my identity as this unchanging background of awareness. The insights, which arise as perceptions, roll effortlessly, the more I am this witnessing:

"I am not the body, not the personality, not the essence, not the mind, not god. I am nothing that is a content of experience. Yet, all experience happens within me. Everything, at all levels, from the spiritual to the physical, happens within me.

I am not touched by any of it. I am untouched and untouchable. I am unchanging. I am deathless. I am unborn. I am uncaused, unoriginated. I was never born, will never die. The concepts of life and death do not apply to me. Life and death are nothing but a process of constant transformation within me. All existence, from the lowest to the highest, is always in a state of flux, but I am the background against which this flux is seen. I am static, unchanging, nonreactive and nonresponsive. I am beyond space and time; both space and time are within me. All of time is a movement within me. Personality, or more accurately, the personal consciousness or soul, is time. Time is the flux of this personal consciousness. Essence is timelessness. I see time as the movement of the timeless in me. All of time, the time of the body and of all of physical existence, is a small process within me. I am beyond time and timelessness. I am the beyond, beyond all and everything. Mind is within me, small and always trying to grasp me."

The silence is vast and eerie. There is a sense of ultimacy, of end. It seems that there is nothing beyond it. It is not that the universal witness is the highest. It is beyond high and low. From this silence, the revelation of all essential manifestations of Being arises in a hierarchy within the background of this the vast witnessing awareness. It contains all the levels of Being, so it exists at all the levels. Experiencing the universal witness is not a matter of ascending grades; it is rather an exit, getting out of the whole thing. It is truly the beyond, the unchanging silent background.

Its main characteristic is that it is aware. In this way it is similar to the personal witness, where the personal witness seems now to have been a limited and personal manifestation of it. The personal witness is aware of the immediate environment of the location of consciousness, while the universal witness is aware, in addition, of the totality of the universe, as if from above or from afar. This perception does not include all of the details of manifestation, but rather a general perception, as if awareness has receded backward until all that exists is in front of it. Phenomenologically, the perception is of being an endless emptiness, so vast that the whole of existence is a small manifestation within it, seen in general outline as a river of images in constant flux. The awareness is aware of itself as a witnessing of everything without being involved in anything. A dark awareness, but not exactly black. It is more dark gray, the color of the aspect of existence, but it is sheer voidness. It is not no-mind space, for although it is beyond thought and mind, mind can exist within it.

The strangest thing about this awareness is its relation to time. It is beyond time. This is different from the sense of timelessness that arises when the essential manifestation of Being outshines everything else, where it seems that time has stopped. It is beyond time. It seems to be what is there before time begins, and after time ends, and at all times.

It clearly is a space with more than five dimensions, for it includes the three dimensions of space, the dimension of time, and the dimension of essence that is the presence of Being. It also feels undefinable, in the sense that no concept can contain it. The more one perceives that it is undefinable, the more there is insight about it. The knowing of it arises by being it, as if it is known only by itself. Looking at it from outside it, or more accurately, when it looks at itself, it simply looks like space. Its relation to time, change and awareness is not seen except through its self-knowledge.

The state of the universal witness continues for a few days. I see everything, the house, friends, family, students and situations all existing and happening within my vastness. There is a sense of utter impersonality, totally transcendent impersonalness.

Understanding and realizing the universal witness allows me to see and understand the totality of the personal life. At this point the activity at the forehead intensifies, and insights start pouring out about the connection between the personal and impersonal. This begins as curiosity about the relation between the intimacy space, which feels very personal, and the witness space, which feels utterly impersonal.

Here the diamond-like presence of support reappears as a big lead diamond in the belly. The understanding radiates out from a lead diamond between the eyes. A flow of insights pours out of this awareness, completing itself as the objective understanding of lead, of inertia, of the conditioning of the personal, and of the ego line.

Lead is the will that supports the conditioning of consciousness. But further, the lead pearl is the unconscious will, the support and determination that has always been supporting the ego-line, the ego sense of being a person. Nevertheless, the ego line contraction, even though it is the personality, is also a role. The role is the personal function or work, developed throughout one's personal history, as the individual capacity to function in a particular way. In other words, one is born with a work to develop and do on earth. It is the personal consciousness—which, for most individuals, is the ego-structured personality—that develops it. The witnessing space cannot do it, because it does not do. This means that one has a particular personal role, which develops mostly through the personality developing along certain lines. The personality is conditioned to be a certain way, which in time will manifest the role and its work. An unchanging and inflexible will supports this conditioned personality. The will is inertia, lead itself.

Usually one gets trapped in the personality, in the role, and takes it to be oneself. In fact, one takes the line of contraction to be oneself. However, the conditioning of the personal consciousness is a program that can develop in such a manner that it will self-destruct when the role, its attendant capacities and its work, have developed. It seems this will inevitably happen if the program leads to the impersonal, the silent witness.

Developing one's personal role and work is the same thing as the maturation and individuation of the personal consciousness. This development coincides with the realization of the personal essence, the pearl that Being develops through the friction of the life process.

Few days later...

An insight reveals a further relationship between the personal development and the unchanging and undeveloping universal witness. The personal needs to realize the universal impersonal in order to be free. Otherwise life becomes enmeshment in the particulars of daily life. The realization of the impersonal is not only for its own sake, it is also for the personal to complete its development in freedom. Life is then the personal consciousness experiencing itself as the flow of the realization of Being.

The crystal night,
Crispness in the air,
A shooting star.

Four

Objective Sorrow

A realization as deep as the universal witness has implications that take years to appreciate. Even the ones I see readily take me a long time to integrate into everyday life. The shift of perspective is so profound and total that one might expect it to immediately eradicate all the mental beliefs and habits which remain in ignorance of this perspective. But as one goes about life this perspective reveals that many unconscious beliefs related to it remain, as the new state of being puts pressure on ways of experiencing oneself which are barriers to its more complete realization.

Therefore, a few weeks after the discovery of my identity as the silent universal witness, I find myself in a difficult dilemma. I begin to be aware of some lax in responsibility. I recognize a certain moral irresponsibility, in the form of not being true to who I am as I have been experiencing myself for a few weeks now.

I gradually come to recognize that even though I have been experiencing myself as the impersonal vastness of the universal witness, punctuated by the arising of various manifestations of presence, I continue to operate as if I am the personality. I continue to live mostly as a person of time and memory, in spite of the certain fact and perception that I am the beyond. There is a feeling that I am being insincere, pretending that I am the personality when I know for certain I am the beyond.

My recognition of this insincerity pierces it, and I become aware of a particular familiar state. I experience myself as a kind of structure, a specific contraction all around the body, as if my skin has grown at least an inch thick, but somewhat soft and pliable. I feel empty inside this thick surface, with a sense of being fake, unreal. I recognize this state as the familiar ego-identity, the soul structure underlying the feeling of self, which the personality uses to identify itself. I see the ego state clearly now: an empty shell, which usually indicates the falseness of taking myself to be an image, instead of merely being.

I have encountered this shell every time my identity has been challenged by a new manifestation of Being. It indicates the identity of the ego-self, formed by memory and history. In this state I feel phony, not authentically myself. At these junctures the process usually begins with the recognition of being identified with an ego structure, with the attendant shame and deep hurt. This understanding gradually dissolves the shell, and fully reveals the emptiness. The emptiness feels like a state of not knowing myself, of not having a sense of self or identity. Holding this deficient emptiness with motiveless global awareness, allows it to transform to a peaceful black spaciousness. This space, which has no sense of self, and no concern for its absence, allows the new identity to arise. The new identity is usually a certain dimension of Being, which now takes the center of experience.

Something different occurs in the experience I am relating, again reminding me never to become smug about what I know, even when it arises from authentic experience. I have learned not to anticipate what will arise, for there is no way to second-guess the action of Being.

A part of the shell at the left side of the body transforms, becoming shiny black obsidian. This transformation is breathtaking but brief. The hardness of the obsidian is quickly covered over with a soft sheath, and there appears a physical contraction at the familiar place of the ego line and around the left shoulder.

As the experience develops a solid hardness appears over the heart area, like a large pebble. It seems separate from everything else in my awareness. I can see that the separateness is connected with the physical tension, which makes the pebble feel like a blockage. It strikes me that the pebble is a protective shield over the heart.

For a few mornings, upon waking up, I begin the day with no awareness of the pebble. There is only a slightly soft and cushiony sensation at the ego-line, sometimes at the spleen. I recognize it as a mild manifestation of the falsehood of the personality, giving me the sense of being a person who can interact with other persons. The dominant state, however, is openness and spaciousness. At some point during the day, the pebble makes its appearance at the left side of the chest. By the end of the day it moves to the center of the body, finally situating itself at the subtle center of the mobius, and a certain emotional state manifests.

The arising emotional state is still obscure and vague, difficult to pin down. This process repeats itself for a few days, regardless of the events in my life. I am usually working during the day, and come back home by evening. The vague emotional state is most present and intense at night, when I have time to be alone in my contemplation.

One night I dream of being some kind of thief. I am caught, and am about to be killed. I wake up feeling strongly: "I do not want to be known as bad." I am intrigued: I am certain this strong feeling is somehow connected to the vague emotion I have been experiencing for a few nights. There is something about badness in this current experience, but I do not understand it.

What about being a thief? How am I bad?

The dream does not reveal its meaning for another day. The following night, I am back from work, and have just finished dinner with Marie. I have been aware of the hardness moving slowly towards the mobius, and now, as it arrives at this center, the emotion arises again. There is a difference this time: the emotion reveals itself as a feeling of a strong sadness, depression, or loneliness. As I recognize the sadness and aloneness I become aware of a concern about being rejected and abandoned for being bad. It is difficult to understand the feeling of badness,

for there is nothing going on in my life or in my inner experience that can account for it. After dinner I watch television with
Marie, continuing to be present with the feelings and the concern. The surface mind is engaged and busy with the show on
the tube, leaving the deeper awareness free to contemplate and
inquire into the inner process. I begin to see that to the arising
part of my mind, being good means being what others want; it
means controlling myself to act in ways that will be accepted
by others. Here, the *nous* glimmers slightly, as the realization
arrives that I believe that being bad means being spontaneously
myself, without control or guardedness.

   I remember recent social situations, where I was more
myself and not hiding it, and I recognize that in those situations
I had been feeling a sense of badness. Realizing this, I see also
that the feeling of badness somehow leads to a sense of phoni-
ness. The falseness, resulting from pretending to be the accept-
able personality when I know who I really am, is due to believing
that I am bad if I am completely myself. I pretend to be something other than myself so that I won't be bad.

   This is an unexpected development—the reverse of the
shame of being inauthentic. I feel bad for being authentic, for it
is not what others want me to be. Seeing this reveals an obscure
identification from early childhood, in which my parents and
school teachers inculcated in me that being good is a matter of
being what they wanted me to be. So to be myself authentically,
which happens every time Being manifests as my identity, always
challenges this identification. And to be the universal witness is
not only to be something that others do not accept, it is being
something they cannot even imagine.

   The emotional state deepens, transforming to something more complex. Now I feel a slight sadness, a strange gloom
and a depressed quality. I am aware of the soft cushiony sensation of the false personality, and a painful feeling of frustration, right at the left side, under the pebble. These feelings reveal
themselves to be a consequence of a deep inner conflict. I do
not want to displease anyone. I do not want to be a cause of pain

to the people I care for. At the same time, I deeply value and want to be myself, whatever this happens to be. I love to simply be, with the freedom, profundity and exquisiteness of the state of simply being. So there is sadness and hurt both ways, for myself and for the others. No wonder there is frustration in the experience. The sadness becomes mixed with the warmth of loving kindness, but some frustration remains.

The next day...

The awareness is mostly lightness, space and lack of concern. When curiosity arises about what happened to the hardness, I become aware of the left side of the chest feeling like a big hard pebble, covered with a soft film. The pebble is bigger and moves quickly to the center of the body, with a deeper sadness that now pervades the consciousness. By evening the sadness transforms to a much more intense state, which is not exactly an emotion. It is an unconditioned state of consciousness, an aspect of Essence I am not very familiar with. It is not exactly sadness, not exactly heaviness, not exactly compassion, not exactly pity, but something similar to these more familiar feeling states. The state seems to be more of an intense and deep sorrow. I do not feel sorrowful, exactly; I am rather aware of the presence of sorrow. As the consciousness opens up, it manifests a deeply golden brown liquid presence, characterized by a profound depth and an intense warmth. Yet, the affect is unmistakably a real, objective sorrow, consuming in some new way.

The inevitable question fills my consciousness: Sorrow about what? Concerning what?

Not clear.

This night, it happens that my friend Karen is visiting me, and as usual on these occasions, we discuss the latest in our discoveries. I describe to her my observations in the last few days. When I describe my present state of poignant sorrow, which has by now been eclipsed by awareness of the pebble, she sees that the pebble looks like a black diamond-like presence, with a layer of brilliant radiance covering it. I cannot at this point see the blackness of the presence, but I can feel that the hardness has a sense of lightness mixed with the sorrow.

The n*ous* begins to radiate brilliantly, with a deep golden hue. The insight emerges: the sorrow is about the feeling of badness, and the conflict of being myself and how it causes pain, for others and for myself, even though it is a selfless movement towards truth. The sorrow is about human suffering, mine and others', and about leaving it behind. It is also about leaving the human personal sphere, as I move deeper into the mysteries of Being. I do not feel that those I am leaving are strangers, for the human sphere represents in a deep unconscious manner my mother, the first human I had known and loved. I see that the sorrow is about the unavoidable suffering, real and imaginary, that results from the process of realization. There is sorrow whenever the movement towards the truth causes unavoidable difficulty for myself or others.

The sorrow is also about the conflict, and most fundamentally for the insincerity that I have been experiencing when I pretend I am the personality. It is also more universal: it is sorrow about the insincerity towards which ignorance so mercilessly drives most people.

As I am fully present in the contemplation of this universal sorrow, I notice that something changes in the state. The conscious presence now attains a different quality, still golden brown, but more golden and more transparent. It feels more like an austere love, sweet but not soft. As I become aware of the subtle taste of this transparent bronze manifestation of Being, which flows like a nonsticky honey, I become filled by a sober sense of sincerity. The sorrow and the sincerity turn out to be phenomenologically very similar. The sincerity has a lightness, sweetness and luminosity that distinguishes it from the sorrow.

The sincerity intensifies the sorrow, and the sorrow becomes a denser fluid and more dark brown in color as the feeling deepens. As the feeling intensifies it almost becomes black. The state of sorrow seems sometimes to intensify so much that it devastates the mind, disintegrating it. It becomes difficult to focus attention on the feeling in the presence.

The next day...

Upon waking up this morning, I sense that the whole body is pervaded with the hardness. The consciousness now has *become* the pebble, indicating the cessation of resistance against it. As I realize this my vision opens up, and a flash of seeing brings me into the depths of the pebble. I see a dazzling blackness, beautiful beyond description. I behold my presence as so deep it is black. It is so black, so pure in its blackness, that it is beautifully dazzling. It is not like the black aspect of essence, which is dazzling because it is luminous from within. This is not luminous from within. It is black through and through. It is so sable black it is brilliant. However, its brilliance is not white or golden, as usual with the luminosity of other manifestations of Being. Its brilliance itself is black. It is so absolutely black it radiates black luminosity.

The presence continues to be hard, and sometimes feels harder than anything else I have experienced. It has the form of a faceted jewel, like an obsidian diamond. This gives the hard presence a texture of sharpness and precision. Yet it is deep and totally empty, not only perceptually, but also in terms of its feeling. This manifestation of Being makes no sense to the ordinary mind; it is like a faceted voidness, which feels within it as an endless still depth of black transparency. I remember what Karen said she saw the night before, and as I feel my deep valuing of her, the obsidian diamond acquires a softness, a pliancy at its faceted surface. I perceive the softness as the pearlescent substance that indicates personalness.

The obscured softness of the false personality is gone, and in its place the pliable, authentic fullness of the personal essence has appeared. I am the total blackness of the depths of Being, beyond all existence, and yet I can be personal.

Being possesses such perfect intelligence that it eclipses what we ordinarily know as intelligence. It responds to the needs of the soul in such complete and unexpected ways, with an aesthetically beautiful precision. In the process I have just described, Being manifested in such a way as to exactly resolve and heal the conflicts and the ignorance. It revealed the need to be good, in the sense of not causing pain, and resolved this situation and healed it, by manifesting essential sorrow, when I realized my helplessness in preventing such pain. It resolved the question of feeling phony and insincere, by manifesting essential sincerity. It replaced the empty shell, the identity of ego, with the radiant faceted blackness, as the depth of identity with Being. And then, it completed the healing by manifesting the pearlescent quality, the personalness of Being, which replaced the fake personalness of the ego.

Clearly, it was the absence of personalness in the universal witness, which is the specifically impersonal dimension of Being, which brought up the conflict around leaving the world, others, or mother. The radiant blackness with a pearlescent sheen is a particular resolution of the issue, for in it I am beyond the world but can relate to it in a personal way.

I could never have imagined such a resolution on my own, using my personal mind. Without the loving intelligence of Being the mind is hopelessly lost. It is also significant to see that Being resolves and heals not only through conceptual understanding, but also, and mainly, through manifesting the necessary states and qualities. This is intelligent grace.

The next day...

The obsidian arises in the morning meditation, but it is partially obscured. I experience it as a shiny black rock over the heart area. Awareness continues, a global holding of all content of experience. The presence of the *nous* feels like a gentle tingling filling the forehead. At some point, awareness discerns anxiety under the black rock, and some concern about my motivation being misunderstood. I recognize the concern is in anticipation of a public lecture I am scheduled to deliver at night. I am not used to giving public lectures, or holding public events. The anxiety and concern create a physical contraction that turns the blackness into a rock. It is like an obsidian diamond in the rough.

Curiosity arises about the concern regarding motivation. However, investigating my intentions in giving the lecture, I realize I have no motivation. The spontaneous inquiry, which is an expression of the presence of the *nous*, reveals that my mind does not accept that I have no motivation regarding this event. So it projects some misunderstanding onto others.

By afternoon I find my awareness inside the state of the black rock. It is a rock no more, but a radiant black crystalline nothingness, that feels like the very essence of the state of peace. Contemplating the mysterious peaceful emptiness I feel a complete aloneness, a total disengagement from everybody and everything. As the black faceted presence I experience no concern in relation to anyone or any idea. I am a truth-consciousness, a presence totally independent from and transcendent to any relation to anything. I am the presence of total freedom from having to respond to anyone. Inner object relations are entirely absent, bringing a sense of complete freedom from all external relationships.

There is no motivation for doing anything, even helping. Nevertheless, there is selfless helping, because the truth is the source of love and compassion. I cannot help being helpful, because it is my nature to be a source of generosity and giving. The crystalline voidness is complete absence of self-centeredness, and this is the essence of selfless generosity. I recognize that this is not my station *(a state that is permanently available)*, but is only the state arising today. I am sure that at some point a manifestation of the personality will arise that will limit the selfless generosity. What is certain, however, is that this state is arising today because I truly have no motivation when I give a public lecture.

The world is but a dream.
A bird on a tree,
That is absolute reality.

Five

End of the World

Four days later...

Awareness is gradually attending to a particular vague feeling that has appeared occasionally for the past few weeks, arising as if out of nowhere. I have not given it much attention, since it does not make sense to my mind. The feeling is combined with a thought. It is as if it is an idea that I feel, instead of think. The feeling-thought is that the world is coming to an end. I have heard many stories of spiritual teachers and psychics predicting the end of the world; my usual reaction is a shrug, not knowing how to make sense of it. If I respect the teacher, I interpret the prediction as a misinterpretation of some inner perception.

I am with a small group, at night, discussing certain aspects of the teaching. I begin feeling the sense of the world coming to an end. I continue teaching, with a small part of my attention on the feeling. The feeling-thought transforms to a perception, an inner vision that now commands most of my attention. I see the whole universe, on all levels, getting smaller and smaller, until it becomes a point. Then, puff, the point is gone. Everything disappears, and only the silent witness remains.

This vision is transposed on the immediate scene of the small group of students in a relatively large room, engaged in heated discussion. It occurs while I am talking and responding. When the vision is over, it leaves me as the empty vastness of witnessing, a pure awareness of the immediate situation, including a dispassionate awareness of the individual me. The experience is more a perception than a vision, for it ends with me actually becoming its finale, the universal witness. It is a very fleeting experience, but leaves a deep mark on the mind.

It occurs to me that this experience is somehow connected to the completely black diamond, but this is an obscure intuition, not a clear insight. What is certain, however, is the feeling-understanding that the total experience of the universal witness is revealing further implications. I understand, experiencing myself as the silent vastness at the end of the vision, that realizing this dimension of identity involves not only going beyond the personal life and history, but also experiencing oneself as beyond all of existence.

What does this mean, however? Is existence something I need to or can go beyond?

As the inquiry takes this direction I remember a small detail of the experience: As I saw the whole universe shrinking to a point, I simultaneously felt a network of subtle physical tensions, mostly on the left side of the body, including the ego-line, concentrating into a point at the mobius. At the instant the universe became a point in my vision, the subtle tension network collapses into a point at the mobius. The collapsed center of tension totally dissolves as the point disappears. At this instant I find myself as the vast silence of awareness, boundless and centerless.

Does this mean that the world that has disappeared is only the universe of the ego-self? What does it mean when the experience is comprised only of the silent witness, with the sense that the world is not? In the fleeting experience, the silent witness experiences the world as not. The experience-vision is definitely that the world is ending. The awareness witnesses an "event" of universal annihilation.

At this point of the contemplation, I become aware that the mind assumes that this disappearance of the world is only the experience of the witness, and that at other levels the world still exists objectively. This makes rational sense, since I continue to perceive the immediate manifestations of the universe. The universe has not actually disappeared, although a sheer luminous awareness now suffuses it. Nevertheless, the inner vision is an actual experience that means something significant, for I feel my mind very deeply affected. Something has annihilated, which is clearly related to the total structure of the personality. But how does this relate to my experience of the actual universe?

This silent inquiry proceeds in tandem with the teaching situation in the room. The state is the sheer emptiness of witnessing awareness, with the *nous* glimmering intensely, luminating with various bright colors. The forehead tingles deliciously, sending ripples throughout the whole head. The inquiry combines the contemplation of the present state, the memory of the recent vision, and insights gained in previous experiences, in a process that utilizes both direct perception and the thinking activity. The *nous* expands as the inquiry intensifies, its faceted clarity merging into the vast centerless awareness of the witness.

The question now takes another twist: When I, as the silent witness, see the world of space-time as within my vastness, is it the real world that I am witnessing, or is it the mind's image of the world? Or are both the same? The inquiry arrives at a silence, in the realization that I do not have enough objective information—direct knowledge from personal insight—to answer this question. Silence pervades the room.

A few weeks later...

The answer arrives through a greater appreciation of the completely black diamond presence. One day the diamond-like presence reemerges as completely black, but now its inner emptiness is utterly complete, revealing itself as total annihilation. Sensing the hardness of the presence, I experience it as a sharply faceted diamond-like density. Feeling its emptiness, consciousness totally disappears, with no awareness left. In other words, contemplating the sense of emptiness coemergent with the presence, consciousness ceases.

When consciousness returns it has the fresh and precise clarity of the faceted form. The understanding which manifests does not feel separate from the sharp, faceted presence. The precise faceted form of presence discloses itself as the precise understanding of cessation, the annihilation of consciousness.

The identity with the personality, or ego-self, is annihilated when I realize myself as the silent witness, or any essential manifestation of Being. However, the identity of the personality does not completely annihilate without the world itself annihilating. This is because the personality and the world are inseparable; they constitute one general object relation. More precisely, the ego-self, with its identity, is a psychic structure that is always in a relation to another psychic structure. The latter is a mental image of the universe, the world view that the mind constructed and developed simultaneously with the ego-self. The ego-self not only swims in an inner social atmosphere of object relations with other people; it also lives constantly in its own world, which is indistinguishable from the way it perceives the "real world." Thus what I usually think of as the real world is not the actual objective world, but the world as I see it through the filter of my inner mental construct.

It is clear now what was occurring in the experience-vision a few weeks ago: what was annihilated was the mental construct of the world. It collapsed to its center, which is the identity of the personality, which then annihilated. This indicates that the ego identity is at the center of the mental construct of the world.

What was annihilated is not only a mental representation of the universe; it *is* the world as I had known it. I had never before known the world directly, perceiving it without the representations developed during my personal history. This world that the ego-self knows and inhabits is truly a mental world, a dream.

As this understanding arises, the black diamond presence expands, filling the house with a magnificent peace.

I have subtle glimpses of the real world, but it appears shrouded in mystery.

The day breaks through me.
I am a window in the universe
For the nameless reality.

Six

The Real World

The inner process accelerates, bringing forth deeper and subtler manifestations of Being. The creative dynamism of Being unveils its various perfections in an inherent pattern. This pattern discloses an order that satisfies my explorations, at the same time transforming my experience of myself and the world.

I am not only an enchanted captive audience, not only a responsive recipient of Being's transubstantiating grace, but also a happy participant. My love for the truth quickens Being's dynamic creativity. This love, sometimes passionate and consuming, sometimes serene and mature, expresses itself as appreciation, openness and surrender to whatever form or formlessness in which Being presences itself. This love deepens my natural curiosity, which manifests as playful but serious exploration, in an inquiry which often takes the form of fundamental questions about existence, but is at the same time passionately personal.

The potential of Being continues to be unveiled in the form of mysteries, disclosed not only as the nature of being but also as dimensions of my nature. Through the revelation of its secrets Being satisfies my heart-felt questions, and also shows me how little I know. Every revelation leads to further questions, in a living unfoldment of my soul. This dynamic process involves both feedback from deeper levels of Being to my inquiry, and a "feedforward" process as I continually ponder the significance of what is being revealed.

A poet said it thus: "always a beautiful answer, that asks a more beautiful question."

The unfoldment of the soul is an adventure full of thrill and terror. It magnifies various life conflicts, as it discloses the essential manifestations that resolve them. This process exposes character deficiencies, ignorance, and wrong beliefs and positions. It involves intense pain, rage, terror and uncertainty. For one who truly pursues truth, however, these difficulties are not obstacles but occasions for further revelations of truth. Inner conflicts and difficulties always turn out to be caused by ignorance.

Being, the ground and source of all that is, has by this time disclosed to me my personal nature. In the realization of the universal witness, it has begun to disclose the nature of the world. This realization has shown me that my experience of the world had not been direct, but had been mediated by my personal view. Understanding this led to intimations of what the real world is, unobscured by mind. This involved answering some fundamental questions, which I was able to formulate only in retrospect:

How is the universal witness connected to the world?
What is the real world?
How is the individual soul related to the real world?
What connects the individual soul to the silent witness?

Experience has taken my identity to the silent unchanging witness, and shown that both the world and the individual have their being in its vast emptiness. I see that my individual self and the world this individual lives in exist in the silent vastness, similar to how physical objects appear in physical space. The world appears as a dream, a mental content, through a perception of duality of manifestation and space.

I felt ill at ease with this realization, knowing that it could not be the full picture, since it did not fit with other knowledge. For example, I was aware of the individual as the personal essence, a person of presence. This manifestation of Being, living as a personal presence, undefined by and free from mind, demonstrates that what exists in the vastness of the witness cannot all be simply mental fabrication. As a person, I am a real presence. So even though I perceive the manifest world as a dream, I wonder, can there be a real world, a world of presence?

This contemplation of the possibility of a real world arose only in occasional hints and subtle intimations, not with any force or clarity. I was too fascinated with the integration of the various qualities and dimensions of Essence, and most recently by the realization of the universal witness, to fully entertain these questions. Nevertheless, Being opened up with full force, disclosing its boundless dimensions in a pattern that revealed the real world. The dynamism, intensified by my passionate embrace of its revelations, had gathered such a momentum that it divulged the beauty and harmony of the real world, even though I had only a dim awareness of such possibilities. Being was responding to my passion as a lover does when he ascertains that he has attained the heart of his beloved: by giving himself totally and unreservedly.

At the beginning of a year of breathtaking revelations, Being disclosed the underlying nature of the world as love. Love was revealed as the authentic body of the universe. The manifestation of Being went further, unveiling its body as pure and undifferentiated presence, in which the particulars of the world are seen to be simply differentiations of this supreme presence, unfolding in beautiful patterns. It divulged the nature of these differentiations as concepts within its spaciousness. At the same time it became clear this presence is both fullness and emptiness.

The revelations continued, with increasing subtlety. What was revealed next was the nature of the world as beyond the mind. Being unveiled nonconceptual clarity as *the truth of the world, in which the world is nothing but the nonmental concepts as and through which Being manifests. The particulars of how the world appears turn out to be nonmental forms, luminous designs inseparable from the total freshness and clarity of Being. To the ordinary state of mind these forms veil the nature of Being, because we experience them as objects. In this realization the forms become infinite beautiful windows revealing the clear luminous nature of Being.*

Here it is sufficient to describe one representative experience, to indicate the quality of this unfoldment. We only need a glimpse of this segment of the unfoldment—the clear day's journey—for us to appreciate its characteristic flavor.

It has been about a year since the realization of the universal witness. A new impression has occasionally been arising, a perception of the world that leaves me feeling I am confronting a profound mystery. There is a sense of wonder, of awe and of a profound ignorance.

I feel that in some basic way I do not know anything. I see, I hear, I sense, but I do not know what I behold. Everything familiar in my life, everything in the world that I have known, all seems so unfamiliar, so unknown, so new, so unfathomable. Nothing has changed externally; the world is the same. But everything seems new and unknown— the houses, the streets, the cars, the people, the sky, the earth, the birds, my family and friends. Even though they have not changed, and I can name them and interact with them as usual, I perceive that I have not truly known any of these phenomena, not fundamentally.

I am struck by how deeply I have been asleep, in a kind of hypnosis, believing that I know what I perceive. But what I know is not what I perceive. I look around me, at the walls, the furniture, the rugs, and I behold a mystery peering at me through everything. I realize I do not know the wall, I do not know the carpet. What I know about them are only bits and pieces, surface qualities: colors, shapes, textures, functions. But does this mean I know them, know intimately and directly what they are?

I realize that I usually assume that when I perceive something, a chair for example, I know it. But now it is as if that assumption is a kind of veil. I look at a chair at the corner of the room. Do I know it? How do I know it? What do I know about it?

What I know is merely a description, is nothing but words and concepts put together by mind.

What do I know about this chair when I say it is big? Do I really then know this chair, or is it that I am aware of some comparison, which takes place only in my mind? When I know it is an iron chair, what am I really knowing? This is merely knowing a word, iron. This word puts together in my mind various characteristics, like hardness, texture, coldness perhaps. But do I know what iron is? I know it is a metal, of a certain atomic weight. I know it is made out of atoms, protons and electrons, and so on. Does this make me know it any more truly? I know concepts in my mind, and that is it. I have never experienced protons or neutrons, and I am not experiencing the iron now. I see only the painted shape, and think that there is iron underneath the paint. I am not even touching the iron of the chair, but I usually assume that I know it.

It is clear that there are different types of knowledge of the chair. There is the knowledge that comes from hearing and reading. There is the knowledge resulting from previous experiences with this chair and other chairs. There is the knowledge of seeing the chair. And there is the knowledge of actually sitting on the chair and examining it. Nevertheless, even this last kind of knowledge, what we call experiential knowledge, is composed mostly of concepts, associated memories and ideas connected with a few physical impressions in the moment. These impressions do not, taken alone, constitute what we think of as knowledge of the chair. It is clear to me that when I feel I know it I know only a word, at most the concept *chair.* Free from such words and concepts, free from memories and information, a chair is a mystery, profound and unfathomable. When I confront the chair directly, without the mediation of my concepts, I realize that I do not know it. This is true about everything in the world, everything that surrounds me.

Words create,

Words annihilate,

But where do they stand?

There is a sense that all my apparent knowledge of the world, primarily ideas and stories in the mind, is peeling away, leaving something unknown underneath. There is mystery all around me. I feel a profound sense of ignorance. I wonder about life and death, about the life of the body, about everything that I have thought naively and arrogantly that I know. I realize that all life, and all objects and processes in life, are full of mystery. I do not really know anything

The not knowing is not threatening. I accept it with a sense of wonder and bafflement. The center of the operation of the *nous*, at the forehead, feels like an open window, transparent and clear. In this openness the activity of the *nous* is so intense that it feels like a continuous series of explosions. The contemplation, which is bursting with insights, acts on the mind like dynamite, shattering its long-held complacency about its knowledge of the world.

At such moments it seems that the perception sets aside the knowledge of the mind and apprehends things nakedly. The chair now looks like the usual chair I have known, except that this is only the external appearance, which I am now acutely aware of as merely appearance. Everything else, the walls and the doors, the floor and the carpets, the lamps and books, all seem to be appearances, surfaces of something much more fundamental, external facades of a more basic reality. I perceive the chair and everything else around me becoming transparent, as if the shapes and colors have become so luminous that they have lost all opaqueness. And through this transparency, naked reality peers through.

It is clear to my understanding that the ordinary knowledge of the world, the knowledge put together by memory and thought, veils the luminosity of appearances, and makes the various forms appear opaque. This opaqueness obstructs the perception of the underlying reality of the forms, by eliminating their inherent transparency. Thus the world is solidified into something inert and dismembered.

And when the opaqueness is dispersed, through understanding its sources, perception beholds shapes and colors that reveal a reality so pure, so fresh, so new and undefiled that consciousness is totally transported, as if seared from within by a cool Arctic wind.

I see through everything, through the surfaces of the various forms, and behold what underlies everything, what fundamentally constitutes all. I penetrate to the center of the universe, to the real nature of existence. What I behold baffles the mind, shatters it and enchants it beyond all knowing: The universe is one infinite perfect crystal, totally transparent, and absolutely clear. A density and immensity beyond comprehension, a solidity infinitely more fundamental than physical matter. The reality of the world is a solid transparency, a compact emptiness so clear it feels like the total absence of any sensation. This sheer clarity, this solid void, is so empty of mind and concept that it feels exhiliratingly fresh, so uncorrupted that it strikes me as the very essence of innocence. It is the virgin reality, before mind arises, before thought knows, before memory is born.

No mind is a freshness,
A sun of ice,
Radiating brilliant clarity.

The experience is not only visual or perceptual. It includes a feeling of delicious transport, of delight and release, of openness and lightness. It is a freedom beyond freedom, a place where no mind ever treads, where concepts are incinerated instantly with the ice coolness of an arctic wind. This coolness, that seems to pervade all of consciousness, is identical to the feeling of freshness, of newness, of virginity, of purity, of innocence. It is the total ecstasy of clarity.

Innocence stings.
It is like a bare bottom
On ice.

I see that this infinite colorless crystalline presence appears carved everywhere into intricate shapes and designs, luminously colorful and enchantingly beautiful. I perceive this carving to be the forms that constitute the universe, many forms but one appearance. Everything that I can see, everything I have known, is nothing but the external topology of the totally void crystalline presence. The world is not a veil, it is only the appearance of reality. Being, which reveals itself now as simultaneously both absence and clarity, manifests itself through the world, and as the world.

The body has also become a transparent form, part of the luminous surface I have known for years as the world. Inside the body, as well as outside it, shines the virgin reality, the nonconceptual truth. Even as I get up, go to the kitchen and begin to cook, I realize it is the immensity and clarity of the crystal presence which is cooking. The wall, the stove and the pots, all seem to be transparent forms, all outside me, and I am their inner core, a sheer clarity, translucent to the point of nothingness. I am delight itself, moving and cooking. I am ecstatic freshness, cutting the vegetables, and tasting the sauce.

The understanding is undeniable: to content myself with the familiar knowledge of the mind is to be asleep. The knowledge of memory, of word and concept, is obscuration. To unquestioningly accept the familiar world is to kill the real world.

The universe is a luminosity,
A transparency,
A robe for you.

Seven

The Absolute

I am in a teaching situation with a small group of students. The discussion concerns the nonconceptuality of essential truth. I am talking from the state of clear crystalline presence. As is usual, the state expands as I present its perspective; this allows my teaching to be more direct and accurate. As the solid, empty clear presence expands, it loses all confining boundaries. It manifests now as the underlying ground of all existence, a boundless and totally transparent medium of consciousness.

At the moment it dissolves all partitioning and spatial boundaries, it reveals itself in a surprising new way. For several months, I have known it as a colorless transparent crystalline consciousness that is simultaneously clear presence and emptiness. Yet at this moment, when it expands to the maximum, it appears totally dark.

More precisely, the new perception is that when the colorless nonconceptual presence expands, manifesting as the nature and substance of all appearance, this presence moves to the surface. The clear, empty but solid presence is now exterior to me, and a deeper truth is revealed. I recognize myself now as this new, now black, presence, and I see the world becoming my surface. In other words, as all appearance manifests as my exteriority, the clear crystalline medium loses its depth and becomes only the clear surface of the newly arising blackness. The final effect is that the clear nonconceptual presence has transformed into a black nonconceptual presence. The blackness is not exactly a color, but rather the absence of color, like one would imagine intergalactic space before there were stars.

I now experience my identity, which is the nature of everything, as a crystal black absence. I feel myself, my existence, as the immensity of presence, absolutely dense and infinitely deep. Yet this immensity and density feels totally light and weightless, completely devoid of any sensation. It is so empty it is total absence. It is nothing, but at the same time it is dense presence. To describe it exactly, it is radiant black crystalline dense absence.

How can absence, which is not existence, have qualities like radiance and density? This is absolutely paradoxical, but this is my experience.

How does this absence feel?

Like the absence of everything. But this absence of everything is simultaneously the solid ground and nature of everything. The sense of this truth is that it is neither presence nor absence but, at the same time, it combines presence and absence. It feels absolute in its truth and certainty. The sense of truth and certainty are not conceptual; they are totally beyond mind and thought.

I do not discuss this newly arising dimension of Being with the group I am working with. I discuss with students only knowledge I have worked with and studied for some time. The work in the group focuses on the process of one of the students, as my inner experience unfolds to depths I have never envisioned.

All phenomena, all that perception beholds, including the teaching situation in the room, manifest as appearance on the surface of blackness. The visual effect is similar to the glimmering reflections on the surface of a clear pool of water, but an infinitely deep pool.

Phenomena are perceived somewhat differently from how they appear in the dimension of the clear nonconceptual presence. I, the person teaching the group, and everything else in awareness, seem real and three dimensional, and at the same time only an appearance in the blackness. As the state continues, I become more distant from the appearance, as if receding backward or inward from the surface. After a while I see phenomena as an image floating in me, the crystal black absolute. I am blackness, vastness, depth and mystery, and everything is a luminous image floating on the surface.

Insights arise, as the characteristics of this new state of awareness become apparent:

I am more distant from phenomena than in the experience of the colorless and transparent crystalline presence. I am as distant from phenomena as in the experience of the universal witness. However, there is a difference: phenomena appear not only as images in me, but as my own radiance.

I am neither absence nor the universal witness. I am like the clear crystalline presence, a crystal black reality. The blackness is total, absolute. This gives the experience a sense of mystery and magic, a majestic beauty and splendor. The sense of depth is stupendous, and inseparable from a magnificent peacefulness. The peace is itself the presence, which is complete stillness of mind and consciousness. Total transparency, complete purity, and absolute absence of obstruction. The feeling is an indescribable intimacy.

Phenomena are the same thing as the perceiving of phenomena, because of the total absence of time. There is no separate perceiver, no separate act of perceiving. The appearance of phenomena is totally inseparable from the act of perceiving the phenomena. Appearance and perception are the same in this experience. Also, the absolute blackness is where all phenomena appear.

All phenomena and functioning appear to perception. I am not involved in what appears. In other words, I am the silent vast black presence, and all phenomena merely appear in me. They appear in me as the arising of perception. Perception is appearance, which is my luminosity.

The inseparability of perception and appearance relates to a specific characteristic of this new manifestation of Being, different from all previous manifestations. There is absolutely no sense of self-consciousness in this experience of presence.

In other words, even though I experience myself as an infinite black depth, when I try to sense the texture or quality of the presence, I find nothing. In all other manifestations of the presence of Being, even the clear nonconceptual manifestation, there is always a texture of consciousness, a sensation of the presence of a medium. Sometimes, as in the clear nonconceptual pres cnce, the medium is a total sense of nothingness, an openness that is so open it is absence. In the black depth, there is not even a sensation of absence. It is as if the essence of this black presence is absence without the sensation of absence. More accurately, consciousness ceases when it tries to plumb its essence. Therefore, since the essence of this presence is absolute annihilation of consciousness, there is no sense of self-consciousness. There is no looking toward the depth, no seeing inward, no possibility of self reflection.

This also means that when there is no perception there is no consciousness. This black mystery is an awareness so absolute that it possesses no ground to look back at and be aware of. It cannot be an object of perception, for it is the absolute subject. It is absolutely nothing, so there is nothing for it to be aware of when it is aware of itself. It is absolutely being the awareness. This is why the word "absolute" seems to fit it. It has no back. It is the ground of all grounds, the final background. To look backwards only leads awareness back to more superficial dimensions, usually back to appearance.

The world is my front,
My face,
And my back is the mystery.

There is identification with the absolute, just as with the clear crystalline presence. I experience it as my very identity, as the very substance of me. Yet there is no feeling of identity. I am identified with the absolute, without the concept or feeling of identity or self. There is no feeling of I, or identity, just the apperception of the absolute, and recognizing I am none other than that.

It seems that the black pebble at the left side that I spoke about in Chapter Four was the beginning of the manifestation of the absolute. I remember seeing its connection to the death of the world. That was before the discovery of the dimensions of pure Being and the nonconceptual presence as the underlying nature of the world. I understood the question of annihilation when the black pebble became a faceted diamond. Now I see that the absolute is crystalline annihilation, which is the absolute ground of everything.

A few days later...

As Being continues to manifest as its absolute nature, I begin to understand how functioning and doing happen. Whatever I do, I do with total lack of self consciousness. There is absolutely no premeditation. The action and the awareness of the action happen simultaneously, inseparably. Taking the action and the perception of taking the action are the same experience. I recognize this as spontaneous functioning. When functioning occurs without self-consciousness it is completely spontaneous.

The feeling is that the spontaneity is the self, which is the vast blackness. The functioning spontaneously arises out of me, with no self-consciousness, without it ever becoming other than me. I am the source, the black crystalline source of spontaneous action. This is difficult to describe. I am not only the source, but also the spontaneous and non-self-conscious functioning. The universe is the spontaneous arising in me, without becoming other than me.

The sense of spontaneity in action brings such freedom and release that it generates both exhilaration and fear. Inquiry into the subtle fear reveals an unconscious need for self-control, and a fear of making mistakes, of making a fool of myself or being inappropriate. I recognize that my action has always been reserved, even when I thought I was spontaneous. Until now, I have never felt that I could be totally and unreservedly spontaneous, not knowing what I am doing except through the doing of it. The fear arises because I feel I cannot have self-control, for I have no self-consciousness. I do not have self-consciousness not because I feel I do not need it, but because there is no feeling of self to be conscious of.

As the understanding unfolds and reveals the previous experiences that lead me to believe I need to control myself to be appropriate, I recognize how I had learned not to trust myself completely. I learned to believe that my nature is not totally trustworthy. Now I see that the absolute depth of my nature is totally immaculate, and is the purest source of action.

The realization that I am both the pure source of functioning and the functioning itself, results in the recognition that I am both the pearlescent personal essence and the crystal blackness. When functioning arises in appearance, the crystal blackness is imbued with a pearly sheen. The radiance of the absolute glimmers with pearlescent beauty.

The universe is personal,
A beauty,
And you are its majesty.

The pleasures of one who
had thus gone
are unspeakable,
like a tangerine sky.

Eight

Mystical Poverty

I have been exploring the question of real relationships with others, particularly regarding how the negative emotions relate to love. The contemplative inquiry naturally surveys most of my significant relationships, investigating how I experience each relationship, and what determines the quality of each. The main issue turns out to be the mechanism of splitting, viewing a relationship as either negative or positive. More subtly, I observe the arising of aversion and hopelessness when there is negativity, and the arising of hope when there is love and positivity. Through this exploration there develops a capacity to continue to love regardless of the presence of negativity, mine or the other's. The heart is becoming courageous. In this development there is a sense of maturity and objectivity.

Coinciding with this understanding, and more directly as a result of contemplating the developing courageousness of the heart, a certain essential structure begins to manifest. A clear crystalline presence appears in the chest, filling the whole thoracic cavity. It first appears as a tall dome-like structure, sitting in a large lotus. The presence feels hard like a crystal, but there is also the sensation of clarity pervading the chest cavity. This clarity imbues the crystalline solidity with such lightness that it feels empty. But it is not merely an emptiness, or a solid emptiness. The emptiness is so light it feels like total absence. In other words, the crystalline presence, although it seems solid and substantial, simultaneously feels as absolutely nonexistent. In fact, it feels like a solid clarity that is so clear that it is paradoxically absent. More particularly, it feels like the absence of anything in the chest. The chest cavity feels so empty and clear that I can only describe it as a total absence of anything that can be felt. The chest is a totally clear window.

It is as if the consciousness is so clear, so free from impediments and obstruction that there is nothing for it to sense or see. The sense of absence brings a sense of total freedom and release, and a lightness that transcends the concepts of lightness and heaviness.

The crystalline structure in the chest has the same quality of consciousness as what I have been experiencing as the nameless or nonconceptual transparent nature of everything. This same clarity of being is manifesting now as the nature of the heart. It feels quite different from how I usually experience heart, so different that it is difficult for the mind to accept it as heart.

How can heart be so empty that it feels like the very presence of absence? All this time, I have known heart to contain the very richness and fullness of Being.

It takes several days of contemplation, with curiosity and openness of mind, before I begin to understand the crystal structure, the crystal heart. This inquiry takes me through a process of becoming aware of a region of my soul that I have never seen so completely or so graphically. I become aware at some point of a certain unclarity in my consciousness that reveals, upon inquiry, a thick and opaque part of my soul. I feel, mostly in my belly and pelvis, some kind of a blobby structure of soul that appears polluted, dirty, almost nauseating. The first reaction is disgust and repulsion, but because of the presence of the crystal heart, and my true desire to see the truth of the situation, I am able to hold this arising manifestation of my soul with an open and inquiring mind. It becomes clear that the turbidity and obscuration in this soul structure is due to a constellation of desires, impulses, needs and wants.

This is a particular manifestation of the soul, the individual consciousness, that is structured by the patterns of identification originating from the oral stage of development, in the first few months of life. Some of the sources of this manifestation of the soul might be inherent to the soul, due to its physical orientation, and because of its lack of development and refinement. The consciousness arises here as an animal organism, ruled by instinctual desires and dominated by animal cravings. This manifestation of the soul is exposed fully only after a long process of refinement and clarification of consciousness. Once the more superficial ego structures become transparent, previously unconscious, very deep soul structures are revealed, structures associated with the instinctual parts of the soul. This level is patterned only by the most primitive ego structures, originating from experiences in early life. Inquiry into this manifestation reveals it to be the libidinal soul oriented towards external sources of gratification, an orientation that automatically alienates it from the truth of Being. This alienation is always present unconsciously, but at some point can be seen and felt directly as a deficient, hungry emptiness, inherent to the libidinal soul.

Investigating this manifestation while experiencing it as a primitive structure of the soul, I recognize that its main quality is attachment. In other words, this nauseating-looking manifestation of the soul is the repository of all my attachments, in the various areas of my mind and life. I see these attachments very clearly. I see the state of attachment, the objects of attachment, and my hopes and desires regarding them. I live with this explicit manifestation of my attachments for several days. As my understanding regarding the various attachments and their dynamics and effects grows, the crystal heart reveals its nature and function.

In this process of investigating the crystal heart and the soul region of attachment, the *nous* attains a crystalline quality;

now it can operate with concepts and beyond concepts. The clarity of the *nous* attains a freshness, and its spaciousness becomes a light-hearted absence of sensation. The sense of transparent clarity and precision dominates the glittering dance of colors, as the understanding goes beyond the qualities and into the fundamental nature of things.

I recognize that in the crystal heart there is complete absence of ego tendencies. The heart is crystal clear, without the slightest movement in any direction. In this state the heart is a manifestation of the nonconceptual clarity of Being: open, virginal and refreshingly cool. It has no position, negative or otherwise. I recognize this state of the heart as true detachment. I experience detachment from everything: relationships, pleasure, comfort, security, knowledge, essence, realization, enlightenment, ego, suffering, and so on.

The state involves a much more total letting-go than does the state of aloneness. Just as aloneness is a more complete freedom than separation, so is detachment a greater liberation of the heart than aloneness. In separation, my experience of myself is separate and autonomous from my experience of other people. It is freedom within the experience of relating. Aloneness emphasizes detachment from relationships; it is freedom from having to have relationships. I am myself regardless of relationships, whether there is relating or not. And since most of my attachments are to things involving relationships, I have been seeing detachment in terms of aloneness.

This new detachment is from more than relationships; it is detachment from everything. Detachment includes aloneness, but goes much further. It is the absence of hope and longing for the objects of attachment, and for the pleasures and comforts they promise, without rejection or judgment. There is full openness to enjoy what is present to the heart and consciousness, yet when an experience is over, consciousness does not dwell on it. There is absence of clinging and mental preoccupation, before and after an experience of enjoyment.

As this understanding clarifies my consciousness, the crystal heart fills both chest and belly. I feel more accepting of the heart in the clear crystal form. As a result, I can see it more fully, recognizing details I have not seen before. Its foundation is crystalline silver and gold, indicating the presence of personal essential will, and essential truth, both beyond concepts. That night, it manifests other qualities, qualities I am already acquainted with as those of the heart. I see the beautiful colors of gold, pink, yellow, grenadine, turquoise, amber, orange, apricot, honey, and so on, as flashings of the facets of the crystal heart. Perceiving the dance of these crystal clear colors, I taste the various kinds of sweetness these heart qualities possess.

I notice that this manifestation of Being arises in a space both black and clear, where the clarity and the blackness alternately dominate.

The crystal heart is now a complete heart, whose essence is clear transparent detachment, and whose manifestations are the sweetnesses of the various forms of love.

A strawberry infinity
A delicious eternity
That is the heart.

A couple of days later...

The inquiry into detachment continues as I learn more about the crystal heart. Today, it focuses on my attachment to the opposite sex. I have had this attachment all my life. I always felt that I loved women, I always wanted to be with a woman. It began with my mother, and now I am with my wife. I am happily married, and fulfilled. Nevertheless, I am aware of a strong attachment to being with her, and having physical contact. I remember how much I have always loved sleeping with the woman I am with, and how greatly I enjoy feeling the warmth of the skin contact. This love and enjoyment reveals a deep attachment, a profound desire for contact, specifically for the female body. The attachment divulges a deep ego structure, which appears as the return of the ego-line in the form of a plastic tube full of the gooey substance of the false personality. The sense of plastic indicates hope for the satisfactions that this attachment promises, a hope based on the false beliefs of the personality.

Tears flood the consciousness, a black ocean of tears. Sadness softens the plastic contraction, and I begin to feel the surrender. I realize the question is not only attachment to sex, pleasure and company. There is something powerful and deep about the desire for physical contact, sleeping together, the physical warmth. This attachment has so far felt too powerful for me to resist. It is becoming clearer, however, that not only these satisfactions, but even their promise, is paltry. The pleasure, the warmth, the various sensations and feelings of satisfaction pale in comparison to the exquisite delicacies and delights that only Being can provide.

At first the tears are about aloneness and letting go of attachments. Then it becomes clear that at a deeper level, they are caused by the attachments. The attachments are a great betrayal of Being. They are equivalent to turning away from what is true.

The tears overflow now. They are not about recognizing the need to let go of the objects and promise of attachments, but because the attachments indicate how I have not fully valued the preciousness of Being. This recognition illuminates the awareness that my attachments obscure the value and the preciousness of the inner realm, the land of truth. It is this that hurts me most.

The contraction in the heart melts, allowing essence to arise in delicate streams of exquisite qualities. Instead of a plastic tube, I see and feel a fluid of two colors, transparent amber and white brilliance. The amber tastes sweet, reminding me of the value of Being; and the white brilliance feels exquisitely delicate, expressing its incomparable preciousness.

Yet, I feel this is only the beginning of working on attachments. It is clear to me that it will be a prolonged and difficult struggle.

One night later...

The understanding of detachment, and recognition of the things I am attached to, are deepening into the realization that I have to let go of even subtler and more basic things. The understanding is making it imperative for me to let go of things I have never thought one can let go of. The letting go has to be total. I need to let go of practically everything: a state, a station, fruit of work, contribution, position, recognition, everything.

With this realization I begin to be aware of a deep, deep sadness and grief. The depth of the sadness feels infinite, an endless dark ocean of tears. This letting go allows me to see that I must let go of everything because none of it is mine. I, as the individual consciousness, own nothing, have nothing, am nothing. I feel so empty, so impoverished, so lacking that I cannot claim to possess anything, not even existence. This is not a state of ego deficiency or self-devaluation, and there is no sense of self-pity in it. It is a heartfelt, immediate realization of a fundamental truth of the individual soul. It is the recognition of the objective situation: the individual self owes everything to Being, for Being is the true source of everything. It is Being that possesses existence, reality, intelligence, qualities, capacities, and so on. I, the individual self, have these available to me only when I am open to Being. On my own, I am absolutely indigent, totally helpless, completely hopeless, thoroughly inadequate. I am nothing but a limp, empty bag.

The sadness deepens, and the tears feel like a dark, cleansing, torrential rain. I am not sad because I must let go of everything that has been dear to me. I am not grieving because I recognize all this does not belong to me, that I am ultimately poor. No, I am sad now about recognizing I have lived a lie, that I have usurped what does not belong to me. The sadness is for the hurt of recognizing that by believing such a lie I have cut myself off from Being, my source and nature. I have estranged myself, throughout most of my life, from the source of all meaning and nourishment, with the ego-pride that *I* have, that *I* possess, that *I* do, that *I* accomplish, that *I* exist. What a lie, and what a shame!

I am sad, but also willing to accept the truth of my situation. I embrace my total emptiness. I welcome my complete, fundamental poverty.

I have nothing. I do nothing. I am nothing.

The state becomes a sense of having nothing, being nothing, feeling nothing, perceiving nothing. Darkness deepens, blackness fills awareness.

At this point, I notice that the indigent emptiness is no longer indigent; I experience it now as an endlessness of peace, an infinity of release, and a completeness of rest.

I realize that by totally welcoming its objective emptiness, the individual self has surrendered its existence into the mysterious depths of the absolute. The emptiness of the self, which I have experienced on many levels as various kinds of insufficiency, and which I have just been feeling as poverty, reveals itself as the complete lightness and freedom of the black crystalline truth. The poverty is nothing but the inexhaustible void, which I have misunderstood by experiencing it through the lie of my independent existence and capacity. As I, the individual self, accept my poverty and relinquish my hold, I in effect accept and embrace the complete voidness of the absolute. Here, I recognize that I am the absolute depth of Being, the source of all plenums.

The infinity of silence is what remains: luminous stillness, absolute transparency, and indescribable intimacy.

> **Vast black sadness,**
> **Hot ocean of tears.**
> **Then,**
> **The unknowable void.**

Prayer:

Oh majesty,
The source of me,
The origin of all,
Absolute ipseity.

May your lightning
Abolish the universe,
And bedazzle mind and heart.
May your mystery
Bring the brilliant night
And annihilate all self.

You are I,
And I am none other than you,
Complete unknowingness
Dazzling darkness
Total presence
In absolute absence.

You are the source
Of all being,
You are the mother
Of eternity,
And you are the beloved
Of the absolutely Poor.
So be it.

Nine

The Beloved

The next morning...

I wake up with the crystal heart filling the chest. I feel it as a hard, neutral presence. I feel an absence of love; this morning the crystal heart does not feel like love. In fact, I feel that I have no heart.

I cannot tell whether the crystal heart feels this way, or if it exposes an ego structure that feels empty of heart. By afternoon, it becomes clear that the absence of heart is not exactly related to the crystalline heart of presence. The lack is revealed to be the reaction of the ego-self. I become aware of a deficient sense of personality.

As I contemplate this conditioned state of the soul, I notice that I slowly become it. I finally feel myself as a person, an ego person with feelings. This clarifies my confusion of the crystal heart with the absence of heart. This person of ego recognizes only familiar emotions and feelings as the presence of heart.

I experience myself now as a person who is not trying to defend or protect himself. The inner condition is naked, exposed. No more defenses, no more pretenses. There are vulnerability, helplessness, weakness, not knowing, some innocence, and a very deep sadness. The person feels all these emotions. The sense of self, with its accompanying emotional state, appears simultaneously with the ego-line, indistinguishable from it. The contraction at the ego line feels harsh and prickly; there is a feeling of deep anguish.

I feel curious about this person whom I have known for most of my life, the person I have taken myself to be for many years. I wonder whether this person wants something.

To my surprise, a longing arises, a longing for the absolute. I see the mysterious blackness of the absolute, and as the empty and helpless person, I feel a definite longing to annihilate into it. The longing arises first as a sad and gentle yearning. Then it gradually transforms into a deep and intense love for the absolute.

The love appears after the longing, as if the longing has been hiding it. The love first manifests as an exquisitely faceted form of presence, a form that combines all aspects of essence in one manifestation. I feel it as intense, pure and selfless love, of various flavors and colors. The sweetness is heavenly, and the appreciation feels so pure it has a sense of divinity.

I realize that many things have been preventing me from recognizing and feeling this longing, from becoming fully the person of ego with all of his feelings and emotions. The heart has been slowly turning, directing its love and yearning towards the absolute.

This turning of the heart has produced guilt—guilt for not loving or longing for anything or anyone. I have unconsciously interpreted the shift of libido towards the absolute as a turning away from what I have loved before. This explains the subtle guilt I have been experiencing lately for not feeling that I miss my wife, or my friends, when I am away from them. There has been guilt for not feeling love and longing for the divine being, the unity of Being, which I have loved since I recognized it some years ago. I did not know my heart was turning towards a greater truth.

> By divine being I refer to the unity of being, when the experience is of everything, the whole universe in all of its content and dimensions, as pure consciousness, pure presence or pure love. This is a state of oneness and harmony, the state of the real world, but I differentiate it from the experience of the absolute, which is transcendent to presence

*and consciousness, and turns out to be the inner essence of
the state of oneness.*

There have also been jealousy and insecurity, relating to
unconscious fear that others will enjoy the love of the divine
being, that perhaps I will not stay faithful to it, and that I will miss
it. I recognize this jealousy and insecurity as a reflection of my
early experience, when younger siblings enjoyed merging love
with my mother, and I felt alone and empty. I believed then that
the loneliness was a consequence of my moving towards auton-
omy. The anguished feeling in the ego-line is this negative relationship, full of frustration, hurt, insecurity and guilt.

I realize that this person feels like I often felt before Being
began revealing its nature: insecure, helpless, lonely and alone,
very sad, weak, without love or connection. It is surprising to see
that, at this point of the unfoldment, this person longs for and
loves only the absolute. This is amazing; the person of ego, when
denuded of all defense and pretense, turns out to be a true lover
of the Truth. It is a healing surprise.

Contemplating my inner state, I experience myself as a
thin film of the gooey substance of the personality, stretched over
the tremendous presence of the absolute. Then I become aware
of the world as a harmonious unity of all appearance, a oneness.
I see all of existence as beauty beyond words, full of love and
grace. But even this is only a thin skin; its substance, its inner
nature, is the vast, completely black absolute.

Through my turning towards the absolute, and loving it
exclusively, risking the loss of the divine being and the unity of
existence, the absolute reveals itself as the inner nature of this
unity. The immense silence discloses itself as the self of the
divine being. I recognize that what I love most is the essence of
the divine, the very self of god. It is the divine ipseity, the self of
everything: absolute blackness, complete annihilation, beyond
being and nonbeing.

The absolute is majesty; when it manifests its crystal
brilliancy it also has beauty. The beauty evokes passionate love;

the crystal form of love attains a deep pomegranate color. The feeling is more than love; it is more like bedazzlement. The beauty bedazzles and enchants. I feel a deep devotional and passionate love, and desire for it to take me and completely annihilate me. That is what I have always wanted.

A subtle understanding further illuminates my situation. I see that when I feel increasing longing, devotion and love I become more identified as the person, the one who longs. As the longing person I am only a shell over the mystery, veiling it even while longing for it. In other words, even by loving the absolute I assert myself, as the individual, and thus become a veil over what I love. To completely have the beloved, my love must annihilate me totally.

I can have the beloved when only the beloved is.

This understanding reveals the loving person as a film over the heart. It is the personality showing its bare condition as a somewhat opaque, somewhat soft, layer of soul substance covering the area of the heart. Through the transparency of this personality trace I see a dark emptiness in the heart area, which I recognize as the feeling of absence of heart, or more exactly, of an empty heart. Understanding of this situation of the soul as lover affects this structure by beginning to dissolve it.

As I feel my very substance melting and disappearing, I first experience the state of poverty. The emptiness of the heart reveals itself as the state of poverty, in which I feel I have nothing. The love, however, is too overwhelming to allow me to remain in any limited state, even that of mystical poverty. The intensification of love melts away even the state of poverty, where now the emptiness in the heart transforms into the dazzling majesty of the absolute. The love becomes so intense, so passionately deep red, that after a while I cannot tell who loves whom. Do I love the absolute, or does the absolute love me? The passionate love is the intensity of the annihilating power of the absolute as it erases all but itself.

I, as the soul, behold the absolute appearing in the heart, occupying it as its rightful resident. The heart beholds the absolute as the most beautiful thing my eyes have ever beheld. It is dazzling and intoxicating, so black it is brilliant with blackness. It is nothing, but it shimmers and shines in such a dazzling way that I can see it has a crystalline quality. It is an infinite black crystal absence, brilliantly shimmering. The radiance is so bright it illuminates the cave of the heart the way a lightning storm illuminates the night. The lightning illumination ricochets in the cavern of the heart with such power I can hear it thundering and exploding.

The beloved now claims the heart fully. It has taken full possession of it, as its own throne. The beloved is not an other, it is the true dweller of the heart, my source, my ultimate self, and the ultimate essence of everything.

I am struck by the realization that in this experience I perceive the absolute for the first time in the heart, by the heart. The absolute is perceived inside the soul, by the soul. The heart reveals itself to be the abode of the absolute. More exactly, the heart is the window to the absolute. I have experienced the absolute many times before, almost continuously, but not in the heart, and not through the individual soul.

A new feeling arises, a completely welcome feeling that expresses a deep realization. I feel I am finally arriving home. This mystery, this majesty, is my home, my original place. It is what my heart longs for and loves more than anything else. I realize I have always loved this mystery, and always longed to melt into it, even though I did not know consciously what I loved and longed for. I knew I loved the truth, but I was not aware that the truth is ultimately this inexplicable reality. I see that I have always felt exiled, that I have always been seeking to return home. As I recognize the home of the soul, I recognize the totality of her search and its true meaning.

A few days later...

The dazzling mysterious truth of the absolute continues to reveal itself as the inner nature of the soul and of all appearance. The constant recognition is that this beautiful mystery is the absolute ipseity, that is, the nature, self and essence of soul and appearance. Today, I am aware of the luminous blackness of the absolute underlying everything. Yet I experience a slight distance from it. I feel slightly less intimate with it. I recognize the beginning of duality with the absolute, by merely taking the perspective of being intimate with it or not, as if it is something other. I realize that although I have been experiencing the absolute as my self and nature, the mind continues to think of it as an other, as an object that I, the subject, can be intimate with.

This insight brings more clarity in the head, and exposes a very basic personality structure. I experience myself as the soul, as presence and aliveness, but recognize that a basic concept patterns the soul into a structure. The concept is the notion of entitihood. I realize that I still believe I am fundamentally an entity. I experience myself as the soul presence, but think of this soul as an entity. This observation allows me to feel the presence of the soul as a blobby or plasmatic shell, empty within. Awareness now recognizes a plasmatic presence, the raw substance of the soul, all over the body, while the absolute is within.

> *The soul can be experienced in many ways. It can be experienced patterned by an ego structure—image, notion or concept—so it appears as a shell, veil, tube, thickness, hardness, and so on. It can also manifest as free from structure, and the experience is then of a formless, blobby or watery substance. It can manifest as imbued by its essential nature, and it is experienced then as an alive and dynamic presence. And it can manifest in its basic mode, before any structure or development, and then it appears as a formless fluid presence. This basic substance of the soul is experienced specifically as a plasmatic fluid, similar to the plasmatic substrate of the physical body.*

With the recognition of the soul as a shell around the emptiness of the absolute, its substance begins to dilute and become watery. I feel it now as tears, warm deep tears, as the blackness of the absolute begins to penetrate and pervade it. The soul melts, becoming an ocean of tears and sadness.

As the perception develops, I become the depths of the absolute, aware of the totality of the universe as made out of soul substance in the process of diluting. The state of unity of appearance manifests now from the perspective of the absolute. The universe exists as a beautiful appearance, as the apparel of the absolute. This leads to further understanding of the absolute, what it is, how it affects consciousness. The understanding is that the absolute is divine ipseity, divine essence, the secret, the inner of the inner, the source, the unknowable, the guest.

Annihilate mind in heart,
Divorce heart from all relationships,
And then love,
Love passionately,
Consume yourself with passion
For the secret one.

When you are absolutely poor,
When you are no more,
Then the guest will appear
And occupy his place,
In the secret chamber,
His abode,
The heart he gave you.

He is the inner of the inner,
He is the secret,
He is the guest,
And he arrives
Only at night.

A few days later...

Today, while having breakfast and then driving to a friend's house, I am not the absolute, but the person who is a direct expression of it. I experience myself as a person in the absolute, and empowered by it from within. The absolute expands out, infusing the person, and appearing-manifesting through him. I recognize the absolute as the heart of me, the self of me, the nature of me, and the person that I am is an extension of it. The self and the extension are united; the absolute and the soul are married.

I experience myself as an extension of the absolute only when there is embodied functioning, such as in eating, walking or driving. In other words, when I am simply resting, not doing anything, I experience myself as the vastness of the mysterious absolute. But when I function, do and act, as an embodied presence, I experience myself as an inseparable extension of the absolute. I function then as an organ of action for absolute Being.

In this condition I am mature, completely responsible, totally the center of my life and action. I am total presence. The presence has no veils over it, no defense or pretense. The back is at the front. Nothing, absolutely no part of me, is held back. There is total spontaneity, and absence of self-consciousness.

The experience is total presence; complete involvement; utter openness; and non-self-conscious spontaneity.

The interplay of involvement and spontaneity, presence and absence, is beautiful and deeply satisfying. I am myself, without a feeling of self. I merely function as my own nature. That is why calling the absolute "ipseity" feels more accurate than thinking of it as ultimate reality or truth. It is the ultimate reality that is both the self and the self-nature.

The passionate intensity and fierceness of presence gives this way of being the flavor of a love affair.

The process of the realization of the absolute continues to expose deep components of the personality, revealing other implications of the truth of the ultimate nature of myself and the world.

This process confronts me again and again with the animal states and tendencies of the libidinal soul: insecurity, fear, vulnerability, helplessness, and so on. When I relax, the passionate burning arises, along with the hot tears. Then the ipseity, the luminous crystal blackness, shines through. I again experience this mystery as both the self and the nature of everything. I see the universe as a beautiful appearance, like a luminous veil over the mysterious darkness. Sometimes I see the absolute; sometimes I feel and sense it, as a luminous crystal presence of black clarity.

A particular perception begins to dominate: awareness of the ipseity as the self. The perception is that I am the ipseity, but it is different from any experience of any other dimension. There is no sense or feeling of I, identity, or self. The beingness of ipseity has no conceptual quality. But there is a perception, or apperception, that it is none other than I. It is a perception of the ipseity being the beingness of me, without the feeling of me. The I is not the familiar I, whether ego or essence.

I know it is I because I am it. There is nothing else that is I. It is the sense of complete subjectivity. This is recognizing the subject that is I.

The old man!
ripened,
finished.

Love
is his pillow.
The mystery,
his home.

Ten

Ripening of the Soul

A few months after the realization of the absolute mystery of Being, I become aware of a curious process. This development is very subtle; it has been unfolding for some weeks before I realize that it is a specific process. It manifests as subtle and fleeting feelings, insights and perceptions.

The first conscious intimation of this development is a sense that I am at the end of a stage of my life. I have done what I had set out to do, in inner realization, work, and personal life. There is a feeling of completion, and a sense that I have no more ambition.

Then there appears a large gap, like a big empty space in my life. I am aware of an opening for something new to emerge. The gap is both in time and space, free to be occupied. Arriving home, and coming to the end of ambition, have left me with a great deal of time and space. I realize now how much space and time seeking takes, whether or not one is conscious of this seeking. The incessant seeking crowds the mind and life with a universe of desiring and discontent, and with a multitude of strategies for fulfillment.

I decide not to try to determine what should happen next, not even to figure out what it might be, but to allow the guidance of Being to unfold my life. This guidance has taken me to my essential home, and it will surely let me know what will come next. In any case, this guidance is actually nothing but the insightful discrimination of what Being is presenting in experience.

One night, watching television alone, after the rest of the family has gone to bed, I become aware of a curious orientation of my consciousness. I notice that certain figures and individuals on the television programs attract my attention. Attention seems to gravitate to older people, regardless of what program I watch. I am fascinated and curious about all of these old people, women and men. I experience an intense curiosity about how they look, move, speak, act, interact, etc. My attention focuses on their interests and concerns, as if I am trying to get under their skin, as if I want to see and feel what it is like to be one of them. I am barely in the middle of my life, but seem to be intensely interested in feeling what it is like to be an old man.

This interest continues for several days. I find my attention gravitating to old people on the street, in restaurants, stores, everywhere. I feel an empathy with them. I feel close to them, affectionate, even a kind of intimacy. I appreciate their slowness, their quiet, their wisdom. I am acutely aware of the effect of the years on them, their bodies and minds, and on their orientation and their concerns.

Gradually, the understanding emerges that the interest in old age is an expression of appreciating it as a time of completion, of finishing with one's life-projects, of ripening. I see old age as a time, or condition, of relaxation and settling, and of not wanting anything, not needing to do anything. It is a time of mental rest, of physical relaxation, of letting go of ambition. Desires have exhausted themselves, and plans have been either completed or abandoned.

I feel a longing for this condition, which my mind associates with old age. This longing is accompanied by viewing life in a new light. I see life, with its excitement, projects and ambitions, as a wound-up spring which unwinds slowly. The excitement and ambition are expressions of the tension of this wound-up spring, impelling us, driving us, relentlessly and mercilessly. Old age means to me that the spring is all unwound; no more tension and no more drive, just a mellow settling. There is appreciation of this settling, of this mellowness.

As the subtle process continues, each day brings new feelings, new realizations, new understanding. The longing reveals itself as a herald of an upcoming development. I find myself, at some point, in a period of feeling settled and contented. I live for weeks with a kind of quiet certainty that I have arrived. There is no more need for effort, no sense in continuing the search. This is not a conclusion, but a realization arising spontaneously from the depths, unbidden and free.

The sense is that the progress of my unfoldment from the nonconceptual consciousness, with its unity of Being, to the absence of the absolute, and the ability to move back and forth between being the absolute to being the person who is its embodied extension, has affected me in such a way that I feel no drive to go anywhere. I am home, in a way that only the heart knows. It is clear that what is left of the process of realization is a matter of refinement, stabilization and actualization in life, which is a continuing process. Discovery has done its job; it has lead my consciousness to its final abode, to its source. Now it is only a matter of integration, of learning to live from home.

There arises now a sense of wonder and mystery regarding life and death. Living at home, mystery reveals itself as the overwhelming truth that penetrates and underlies all experience. Life is rich and colorful, but it is only the miraculous unfolding of mysterious Being. Regardless of how much I understand it, I still do not truly comprehend it.

I also keep feeling the mystery of death, that life as I know it will end. Yet it is unfathomable. How can life end? I know it does, but how can something so robust, so conscious, so vibrant, actually cease?

Can life comprehend its own end?

In time, I begin to experience the end of life, as I sink deeply into the mysterious depth of the absolute. Consciousness ceases, perception stops, and there is absolutely no awareness at such times. Yet, when consciousness arises, the question of how death happens is still unfathomable. The cessation of consciousness is not a new experience for me, for it is one of the stages in the journey towards the absolute. Now, however, the cessation is happening as part of a new process and a new contemplation, the question of the mystery of death.

I recognize that the individual consciousness does not have the capacity to understand that it can end, or that it will end. I also recognize that the death I am contemplating is not necessarily only that of the physical body. It is more fundamental. It is the cessation of consciousness. I begin to see death as final, as the ultimate dissolution of consciousness into the absolute. This comes to pass, but the mind still cannot comprehend it.

Some weeks later...

Today the process presents itself as the feeling-recognition that I am at the beginning of a new life, a different life. I feel that I have already lived my life and finished it. The life I have known is over because it is finished. It has run its course, and completed all its initial programs. The journey is over. Arriving home is the end of the journey of life. This ending culminates in a particular death, which is the cessation of the consciousness of the soul in the annihilating space of the absolute.

The life I live now is extra, is a bonus. There is no concern about whether it continues or not, or about what transpires in this life. I have received all that I have ever wanted. I want nothing more. My heart is contented, and my drive spent.

A few days later...

I have been aware that this process involves two intertwining threads—the first a process of finishing and ripening, and the second the contemplation of death. The finishing ends in a certain kind of death, which in turn ushers consciousness into a life of ripening and contentment.

I recognize that all need or movement towards a goal, even towards creativity, is ambition, which is based on ego activity. Creativity can be spontaneous unfoldment, but when it is, it happens on its own. I do not need to move towards it, want it, or concern myself with it.

As the absolute, all that appears to awareness is my creativity, without my lifting a finger. I am the source of all that arises.

The recognition of being devoid of ambition deepens the peace and settling of everyday consciousness. This settling becomes a feeling of contentment. The soul, the individual consciousness, begins to feel like a blobby pearl, soft and pliant, relaxed and settled. It is like being a liquid pearl, suffused with the stillness of peace, and empty of reaction or drive toward activity. Sometimes this feels like being a relaxed old man.

Beyond ambition,
beyond attainment,
is home.
Contentment,
without content;
peace,
uncaused.

The peace and contentment develop into a sense of fulfillment, as the consciousness attains a nectary fluidity, with the sweetness and aroma of apricot nectar. I feel a sense of maturation, not in terms of capacity, but in the sense of ripening. The fulfilled consciousness becomes a ripening when I experience the soul not only pliant and nectary, but full and sweet, just like a very ripe apricot. The whole soul becomes a heart, a heart full of the most flavorful apricot nectar.

This ripening transubstantiates the essential state that arises during the function of teaching.

When I take the role of the teacher, I frequently experience myself as an objective presence with various capacities and facets. There is clarity and maturity, intelligence and a dynamic interplay of various aspects of essence. The state feels like being a full pearl of consciousness with clear sharp facets of various colors. I think of this state of teachership as a diamond pearl. After the realization of the absolute, I have been experiencing this state of the incomparable pearl as a manifestation of the mystery. I perceive the inner identity of the pearl as the mysterious radiant blackness of the absolute.

This state goes through a further development: As I teach a group meeting, I notice my state is the diamond pearl. However, I also feel the sense of contentment, fullness and ripening which has been my general condition for some time lately. The sense of being a juicy ripe apricot arises as the inside of the diamond pearl. I am now an objective and multifaceted personal presence, but relaxed and settled, fulfilled and ripened.

Arriving home ripens the soul, and this ripening is its fulfillment.

This process of ripening interweaves with a continuing puzzled contemplation of death. I keep remembering that I will die someday, but this cannot be comprehended by mind. It becomes increasingly clear that the death I am contemplating is not only physical death, but also the death of the individuality of ego. Deeper still, it is the cessation of all consciousness. I intuit an end, a cessation of consciousness.

This contemplation, however, culminates in an unexpected development. This occurs again when I am watching television. I am relaxed, rested, feeling contented, with no specific reason for the contentment. Unexpectedly, I have a flash of feeling myself as dead. I am conscious, as an individual soul, but I feel dead. It is as if I am a mummy or a corpse. The soul appears as a corpse, and feels like a corpse. This is curious. It is not the cessation of consciousness, but the consciousness experiencing itself as a corpse.

A few days later…

Quietly and subtly, the feeling-realization that I have reached my destination returns. I did not know that it was the absolute that I was looking for; I have been intensely motivated to find the truth, without knowing what the truth I am looking for is. I have discovered many truths, fundamental truths that changed my life, but none of them seemed to spontaneously end the process of search. But when the absolute manifested itself in the heart, there was heart-felt certainty that it is what I have been looking for, without the mind knowing it.

The certainty that I have found what I have been looking for, and the ripening of the soul, have contributed to the process of integrating the awareness of myself as the absolute mystery. For many weeks I have been feeling relaxed and settled in a certain way. There is an ease and simplicity, a contentment independent of the events of the day.

For a few days lately, however, I have been aware of a new development: a readiness to give, an openness for generosity, and space to spare.

The realization of fulfillment, and the sense that my life is a new life, engenders a sense of having lots of time, energy, and space to give to others. I feel willing and happy to give my time and energy to my family and friends. There is nothing that I want, or want to accomplish for myself, and there is a great deal of space. It is not that I am doing less, or that there are fewer physical activities. The sense of space is psychological; my consciousness is much less cluttered.

When I feel the attitude of unrestricted generosity, I am aware of being the absolute, an absence that has no sense of self. This state of being the crystal absence, that has not an iota of self in it, is the core of generosity. I am willing to give energy, time, and attention because there is no self that needs them. The self needed all these, and many other things, to go home. Now that it is home, it is gone, and everything that arises is for others.

I feel I am home now, my search is ended. The absolute is home. My personal motivations have spent themselves, and now it is the dynamism of the absolute that moves the soul.

A couple of weeks later...

The identity has been alternating between the absolute and the soul. As the soul I am human. Whenever I am human, and know what my heart feels, I realize I long for and love the absolute. Otherwise, I am the absolute, an infinite majesty. There is no problem when I am the absolute, for I am the self of everything. And there is no problem when I am human, for then I love the absolute.

The only problem is when I am human and not in touch with what my heart feels.

As a human being there is no sense of being a person, nor is there a sense of not being a person. It is of being human, in a normal way. This has been the dominant state for about ten days now. It is a state of being normal, human, with an open and loving heart, with selflessness and generosity.

I experience myself as the soul, a kind of conscious substance with qualities between the white personal fullness of the pearl aspect of essence, and the plasmatic, clear, basic medium of consciousness.

As the consciousness which is the soul, I appear transparent, and become translucent, sometimes even luminous. My ultimate nature is the crystal absence of the absolute. There is a sense of integration in this experience, different from any other. It is not as definite and clear as that of the pearl; I do not feel I am just a beingness. I am more a human being, an alive, responsive and functioning conscious presence, and at the same time an inseparable expression of the absolute mystery.

Is it the cup,
Is it the drink in the cup,
Or is it the drinker of the drink?
The mystery peers through all.

Eleven

The Mystical Marriage

Regardless of what I happen to be doing—working or conversing, resting or walking—I am aware of the reality of death. Death constantly occupies a corner of my consciousness. I seem to be contemplating death spontaneously, with no conscious initiative. There is no agitation or anxiety, only curiosity and bafflement. The questions arise unbidden: what is death, what does it mean, how does it feel?

I feel certain that one day there will be death, at least for some part of me. I feel as if I am trying to grasp within my heart and soul what death will be like, but to no avail. I feel that death is staring me in the face, yet the whole question of death feels unknowable and mysterious. I keep wondering: is it loss of sensation, is it loss of boundaries, is it loss of mental capacity, because there will be no brain?

I generally feel peaceful and contented. My life is fulfilled and complete. But this completeness and fulfillment seems to be the reason that my consciousness is spontaneously contemplating the question of death. It is not a morbid preoccupation, but a genuine desire to face something significant, in a way I have never dared. I want to know death, for it feels so near. I want to feel it, taste it, touch it, be intimate with it. My soul is a burning question about death.

One night, I am walking through the hallway, coming from the bathroom and going into the living room. The family is asleep, but I have developed the habit of spending time alone at night, being quiet with myself, doing nothing in particular, allowing experience to arise and enjoying the contemplation of whatever Being presents. The contemplation of death is an almost palpable sensation as I walk slowly through the hallway. The contemplation intensifies as I reach the dark end of the hallway. Here I begin to see a blackness. I feel I am walking into a mysterious, veiled blackness, not the semidarkness of the hallway, but a blackness that I perceive through the walls, beyond the boundaries of the physical world. It is as if the walls around me dissolve away, becoming increasingly transparent, revealing the mysterious blackness.

As I continue walking, now slowing my pace, I realize that the blackness that I see in front of me, the blackness I seem to be walking into, is veiled. I see it through obscurations, through what looks like many subtle veils.

The contemplation of death appears to me now as the dissolving of veils. I realize that throughout all these days of contemplating death, I have been going through and dissolving these veils. Each question, each realization, each feeling, each intuition moves the awareness through another veil. I have been contemplating death through the veils of my ideas, and as my consciousness sinks deeper into the contemplation, the deepening of consciousness rends further veils, allowing a deeper penetration into this mystery. Now this penetration reveals a blackness that pierces through all physical appearance.

I am looking death right in the face. I see death everywhere, all around me, penetrating everything. At this point several insights fill my consciousness, creating an overall understanding and furthering the ongoing contemplation. First, I am aware of a direct, spontaneous acknowledgment of my mortality as a human being. Death is certain for me, as I experience myself as a human being.

At this point I am sitting in the living room, with dim lights, and the darkness of the night pouring through the window. The darkness of death feels deeper and much more profound than this darkness of night, but the two become one, and I am enveloped by a deepening blackness.

The blackness peers at me through everything. I begin to feel a curious aloneness, peaceful and poignant. This is what death is: total aloneness. In fact, it is simply the acknowledgment of my already existing fundamental aloneness, the aloneness of Being.

I am alone, in death.

My experience of my existence is all there is, and this existence is the presence of death itself. The awareness now is that the mysterious blackness is the face of death, which is aloneness—a peaceful, pure aloneness.

The aloneness begins to reveal a quality that I do not usually associate with aloneness. I begin to feel an exquisite intimacy, as if the atoms of my consciousness have become its very essence. Death seems to coincide with both intimacy and aloneness. The mysterious blackness of death brings aloneness and intimacy together, joining them into one quality. There is a sweet and delicate intimacy in the heart as I contemplate death and see the presence of blackness.

Contemplating the intimacy and sweetness pervading my chest, I realize that my body has lost its usual boundaries; it is now all of existence. I am the room, everything in the room, and everything beyond the room, all as one presence. The sense of what I am is an immense, adamantine crystal presence, an indivisible totality. This totality which I experience as my body is all of the universe. Also, curiously, at the location of my physical chest this unity of existence is a sweet intimacy. The contemplation of death has led me to the mysterious blackness underlying all of existence, and this has made it possible for me to experience the unity of Being as my body.

The contemplation of death continues for days, each time taking me to the mysterious blackness, and ushering me into the unity of all existence. If all existence is my body, then what does it mean to die? It seems I am learning that death is the entry into the undying cosmic body.

A few days later...

The recognition of my mortality keeps returning: I will not remain the way I am now.

This deepening contemplation mingles with another thread of experiences. I have been noticing various experiences of loss of support. I keep feeling this loss of support in relation to people I have depended on for various things. Situations seem to conspire for me to experience the loss of one support after another, from one person after another. I do not feel any recrimination about these losses; in some sense I am relieved, for I am learning more deeply how I have unnecessarily depended on others for various things. I am aware that these losses are inevitable, for my sense of identity is now with something no one can support. Being is its own support, and the more I recognize it as my very self and identity, the more the supports for the old self fall away. Vulnerability arises, along with a sense that there is no ground to stand on. This becomes quickly a loss of the sense of self; of feeling lost, not grounded, not centered.

These perceptions seem to relate to the confrontation with mortality. This contemplation makes these experiences of loss of support less important.

I realize that the issues regarding support feel important only when I think I will be around for some time. The contemplation of death exposes the familiar sense of self, and dissolves its habitual supports.

This contemplation begins also to highlight awareness of my sensual attachments: to physical and sexual contact, food, entertainment and comfort. I feel unable to break such attachments. Sometimes I feel unwilling to break them, because I still love such things. It seems to me there is something behind such attachments that I do not yet understand, something real.

One evening, driving across the Bay Bridge from San Francisco, the contemplation of death arises. It brings to mind my recent losses of support, the sense of being lost, of having no identity or center. I recall how I am still unwilling to let go of some of the things I love in my life. Unexpectedly, my consciousness submerges into the silence of the absolute. There is now depth and intimacy, mystery and radiance. As this mysterious silence, I see the cars around me floating in the black vastness. The whole bridge is floating in my vastness, including my own car. All phenomena, including the bridge and the night sky, are shimmering appearance arising out of my mysterious depths. This appearance is luminously beautiful, penetrated by the black mystery.

I do not drive, I only witness all appearance unrolling in front of me, including the movement of my car, and the arms holding its steering wheel. It is an enchanted world.

Within this beauty, I am aware of a small part of the soul, to the left side of the body, which is not completely open. Sensing into it, I feel the attachment to, and love for, the sensuous objects of desire.

This focuses my attention on this part of the soul that is still not willing to let go and surrender its attachments. It becomes the beginning of a new thread of inquiry that lasts for a few weeks.

One night I am having dinner with a few friends, and allowing this manifestation of the soul to arise and expand. I notice something disconcerting about it. I see that from within the experience of this part of the soul I am not aware of the preciousness of Being. I am still in touch with the presence of Being, but its exquisiteness, beauty and delicacy are dimmed. Furthermore, in the experience of this soul of attachment, I feel no strong desire for the various exquisite qualities of Being. Staying with this understanding, and not trying to change it, I realize, to my surprise, that I simply love the absolute. I am not interested in any of the exquisite qualities and manifestations of Being. I love only the absolute, the luminous night.

Upon seeing this, I am aware of the arising of a gentle, sweet love, softening this part of the soul. The soul becomes a soft, sweet soul. I realize that I am experiencing the love of the soul for its source, nature and home. As the soul, I sometimes mistake this love for a desire for the sensual objects of the world. Now, I am not any of the exquisite manifestations of Being, I am not the mystery of the absolute. I am an individual being, a soul that loves the absolute. I experience myself as a soul, real in the realm of souls, but conceptual at deeper levels of truth. And this soul is having dinner, conversing with friends.

The experience changes slightly as the love becomes clearer, and welcomed. Aware of the absolute as the depth, the ground, the nature of everything, I see this luminous blackness holding everyone, and holding the dining table we are sitting around. The tablecloth, the dishes of food, the people eating the food, all look luminous and radiant, arising from within the silence. They are the patterned radiance of its own nature. Silence surrounds us; the conversations are patterned sounds arising within it. My mind is empty and quiet, even though I continue to talk.

Curiously, I am still aware of the individual presence of the soul. This state of awareness of both soul and absolute is new. I am not experiencing the two alternately, as I have in the past, but simultaneously. I am both the silent vastness and the individual alive presence, but they are one. This perception is difficult to describe; I am the soul loving the absolute, which is my source, nature and home. The absolute is much larger than the soul, infinite; and the soul is a delicate formation out of it, an extension of it. The soul is almost like an image on its surface. And I am both the individual soul and the infinite absolute, paradoxically comprehended as one.

The two are so inseparably one, as if the absolute is the body and the soul the face of the body. The soul is very delicate, transparent and very much part of the absolute.

The experience is subtle and intimate, and in this intimacy there is delicate love. It is after dinner and my eyes are closed, so it is a completely inner experience, between me and my source, as an intimate marriage.

A few days later...

I remember my initial experience of arriving home, when it became clear to me that the absolute is the true beloved of the heart. I remember feeling that my life as I have known it was over, and a new life was beginning. I did not know what to do with the rest of my allotted time, and I decided to wait for the guidance of Being. These memories occasion the arising of a specific feeling. I begin to feel very clearly that what I want is to live in the absolute. I do not want the rest of my life to be simply an exploration of his kingdom. Being home means being inseparable from the absolute, not just in it.

I see that my function from now on is to be a mouthpiece for the absolute. I am an expression of the absolute, an expression that reveals its truth, its majesty, that speaks from this mystery.

I begin to understand that all the knowledge I have encountered about the soul and its development is secondary to living in the absolute.

> *The discovery of the absolute accelerated the unfoldment of the soul, and a great deal of knowledge was revealed. Before that, Being had manifested many of its aspects and dimensions, revealing a staggering expanse of precise knowledge through the exquisite experiences of the soul. The door of knowledge of Being has been open to me for many years now. All I need to do is to be interested and to focus my inquiring attention on a particular area, and experiential knowledge unfolds.*

I realize that all this experience and knowledge is an exploration of the kingdom, the manifestation of the treasures latent in the absolute mystery. This exploration now is seen to be identical to the development of the soul, leading to its realization of the absolute and its eventual ripening. It is clear that this development of the soul is not only for its development and realization: it is for her to serve the absolute, by expressing it, by embodying it in the world. The ripened soul is the vehicle by and through which the absolute lives and acts in the world. How else could the absolute walk and talk?

I am aware that I do not care for any of the knowledge about the soul and the various manifestations; my love is the absolute. But since as a human individual I have time to live, I will live it by purifying and developing myself in order to become more able and worthy to serve the absolute, and express it by being an expression of it.

The guidance is finally showing me that the rest of my life will be spent in developing and purifying the soul to be a true and complete expression of the absolute, an effective instrument for it. The knowledge gained is for the guidance of others towards the same aim. In other words, I live not for myself, but for the absolute mystery. The absolute is the self that lives the personal life of the soul.

Oneness is dead
God is gone
Everything is as it is.

Twelve

Coemergence

It has been a few years since the discovery of the absolute. The discovery and continuing realization of this mysterious depth of Being has impacted the soul profoundly; subtle areas of experience are deeply touched. For many years the soul had already been going through an intense transformation, under the impact of the continuous unfolding manifestation of aspects of Essence and dimensions of Being. The discovery of the absolute accelerated this already rapid process, and made it possible more clearly to identify the boundaries of that process. The complete transcendence of ego experience in the realization of the absolute illuminates the barriers in the personality that oppose this realization.

This transformation of the soul has been proceeding along two related tracks. The first is the clarification and purification of the very substance and consciousness of the soul, that has gradually led to a maturation and ripening of personal human experience. The other is an increasing integration of the soul into the absolute, in various stages of assimilation and embodiment. This has taken the form of realizing that the absolute is the true beloved of the soul, its home and source. It lead to recognizing the absolute as the inner and absolute nature of the soul, its deepest identity and center. This initiated a particular subtle process of transformation that involved the contemplation of life and death, and *confrontation with various attachments and forces which tend to mold the soul's experience.*

I begin to see that the processes of clarification, integration and confrontation with death are the direct effect of the absolute on the soul, as the mysterious emptiness penetrates the soul's substance, and the invisible light reveals its various hidden corners. The influence of the absolute on the soul exposes ego structures, refines the soul's substance, and metamorphoses its consciousness toward the nature of the absolute. In this process of clarification and purification the soul loses her identification with the historical person and identifies more with the absolute. With this decreasing self-identification based on mind and memory, experience becomes the natural, spontaneous realization of true nature, as nonconceptual abiding.

The more I contemplate my experience of the absolute the more I appreciate how mysterious it is. At first I saw it as absolute being, as the immensity that underlies everything. Yet this immense presence reveals itself as total emptiness, a complete absence of any substance. It is both a presence and an absence, but recently my experience has been focusing mostly on the sense of emptiness. This focus was strengthened by my attending a talk by the Dalai Lama. My consciousness was strongly impacted by his embodiment of both absolute emptiness and loving kindness.

Continuing to experience the emptiness facet of the absolute has exposed new ego structures, which initially become conscious as contractions in certain areas of the body. Inquiring into these contractions reveals contracted manifestations of the soul, related to questions of identity and support for identity.

Tonight, however, I am aware of the intimate emptiness of the absolute, and not of the contraction. But there is something new and curious about the experience. As I feel myself as the emptiness of the absolute, I also feel it as the soul. I cannot separate the absolute emptiness from the presence of the soul. I am riveted to this manifestation of consciousness, inquiring into and contemplating it.

I begin to discriminate more clearly what I am experiencing. I experience myself as the soul, in a very soft, relaxed, ripened condition. The presence is so soft and malleable it is almost nothing, so empty of occlusions and opaqueness it is transparent. I feel transparent to and pervaded by the absolute. I recognize that I am being the soul and experiencing the absolute in a new way. What is new is the relationship between the soul and the absolute.

There is the presence of the soul, the individual consciousness, but she feels herself as the absolute. Even though the soul feels herself as the absolute, which is a mysterious nothingness, she is not completely gone.

Before this experience, when the soul unites with the absolute she annihilates into it. Only the absolute remains, as self and identity. The only way I had experienced the soul present simultaneously with the absolute has been as an extension of it, in some form of dual unity. The greatest of these conditions of integration has been that of mystical marriage, where the soul becomes an inseparable part of the absolute, almost like its face. So the present experience is a surprise.

I realize that this is a new level of integration between the soul and the absolute. I am the mysterious vastness of the absolute, and this vastness manifests a delicate, contented quality of the soul in the location of the body. This delicate manifestation is still the absolute, but with an added quality of presence at a particular location. There is much less differentiation between the indeterminate emptiness of the absolute and the consciousness of the soul than I have experienced before.

This development seems to be a level of resolution of the identity issues related to the soul contraction I saw a few days ago. I have been seeing the identity issue as relating to authenticity, being true to my true nature. Can I experience myself and act from a place where there is very little or no distance from my true nature? The contraction indicated a remaining identification with the historical person of history, which identification functions as a veil distancing the soul from identity with the absolute. The soul contraction I was inquiring into is gone, replaced by this new state. The arising of this new level of integration between the soul and the absolute clarifies how one can be the soul and act from the absolute. This makes it possible to take personal action, without departing from my identity as the mysterious absolute.

The next morning, this realization initiates a new contemplation. In the morning meditation there arises in consciousness the contemplation of the essential personal as an important part of realized human experience. To realize the absolute with its emptiness and mysterious light is not the only possibility. The next step is to be a human person, without losing the realization of the absolute. It is a realization of a particular state of unity. This unity of existence does not blot out personal consciousness. Most traditional spiritual teachings do not have this understanding, or do not give it much attention. I recognize the possibility and value of this integration, especially for living a human life on earth.

As I wave to Marie, my wife, "see you later," on her way out the door to work, I am aware of myself as the vastness of the absolute. The mysterious vastness of the absolute is waving the hand, and feeling personally affectionate.

A few days later…

For several mornings I have been waking up feeling happy, but experiencing myself as an individual. I have been thinking of the experience as that of the ego individuality, but I am seeing that is not so. The understanding fills the soul that even though I experience myself as an individual, it is still the experience of the soul inseparable from the absolute. I am an individual, a human person, but I am still the absolute. Individuation can be a real experience, not only on the level of the essential development of the soul, but even on the absolute level.

I experience myself as a soft, relaxed and ripened soul. I am an individual consciousness which I experience as presence.

I am a living presence, free from contractions, identifications or mental elaborations. I am clear and transparent presence, but feel alive and dynamic. As this presence I experience myself as delicate and exquisitely fine.

The sense of I or identity springs from within, as an innate self-recognition. It originates from the center of the presence, which I see now as a brilliant point of light. The point of light is alive and scintillating, beautiful and precious. Yet, as both the living delicate presence of the soul and the brilliant point of light, I am inseparable from the nothingness of the absolute, an expression of it that is it. I am the absolute mystery, a vastness that has manifested itself within itself as a transparent sphere of conscious presence, whose center is a radiant point of light. The felt experience is lightness and intimacy, preciousness and exquisiteness, and total personal vulnerability.

This is the quintessence of being a real human person.

A couple of weeks later...

Driving to see my friend Karen, I become aware of my presence evolving to a new state. Again the soul and absolute are integrated as one presence. I am aware of the winding road, and contemplating my sense of presence, awareness reveals the integration of soul and absolute to be complete; it is a total synthesis. Contemplation beholds complete coemergence of soul and absolute. The union is much more complete than I have experienced before. This total coemergence transforms the felt qualities of the presence. The lightness is extreme now; it is as if there is no gravity at all. It is the emptiness of the absolute in its total lightness and transparency. And there is an amazing translucence, a clarity that is itself the lightness.

I am aware of soul, aware that I am not experiencing only the purity of the absolute, because there is a subtle perception of a completely clear and translucent bubble of awareness. Along with the indescribable lightness and spaciousness, and inseparable from it, I experience a presence that looks almost like a mirage, an illusory body.

I arrive at Karen's house; and we sip tea as I tell her about my present experience. After a while, she begins to perceive and participate in this coemergent presence. As we inquire into and discuss our perception, the presence expands and includes all of our environment.

All appearances now, all objects in the room, seem to be transparent and empty bubbles. The furniture, the cups, the windows, our bodies, all appear as translucent bubbles of various shapes, sizes and colors. All the bubbles are connected together, like a cluster of soap bubbles. I see Karen as one of the bubbles.

I perceive myself as a bubble connected with the other bubbles. But the bubble is clear and translucent, transparent. It is also completely coextensive and coemergent with the spaceless emptiness of the absolute.

The essence of the bubble is the absolute emptiness, which is more of an absence, or nonexistence. Yet the bubble is presence. This presence is indicated by the barest minimum of clarity or awareness, just enough clarity so as not to disappear into the fathomless blackness. In other words, the bubble is only a glimmer of clarity within the deep darkness of the absolute, but not dual with the absolute.

The soul is a bubble of awareness, and all of the environment is composed of the same translucent clarity, a mere patterned radiance within the blackness, and inseparable from it. There is perception because there is awareness, which is the same as the translucence of the absolute. This awareness of the absolute is the clear bubble-like transparent presence. In this experience there is emptiness, which is more like nonexistence or nonbeing. It is absence. There is clarity, which is transparent and colorless. There is awareness, totally unobscured and translucent. There is lightness, no weight at all, no density.

Within this experience I begin to feel a gentle throbbing at the area of the forehead, a forehead that seems like a mirage. I begin to be aware of the glittering radiance of the essential *nous* at the area of the forehead. It feels as if a portion of the bubble has transformed into a faceted, variegated diamond-like presence.

It feels like a faceted liquid luminosity, glittering and shining. This glittering manifests in cognition as insights related to this new development.

I recall a concern, which occasionally becomes a fear, that complete absorption into and unification with the absolute means cessation of all experience and loss of everything. I thought that total merging with the absolute might mean total and permanent cessation of consciousness, and hence all perception. I could not anticipate what total integration with the absolute might be like. This experience of soul coemergent with the absolute answers this concern and resolves the fear. Everything remains, is not lost, does not disappear. But it is seen not to exist; nonbeing is its ultimate condition.

There is no disappearance, there is only the understanding that no appearance actually exists in the way we usually assume.

The fear of loss is resolved in another interesting way. As I contemplate the experiential qualities of this coemergence, the insight arises that it is actually never possible to hold onto anything in any case. It is not possible to hold onto anything because nothing exists the way it appears. The true reality and condition of phenomena includes nothing one can actually grasp. One cannot grasp a mirage, or a hologram. Furthermore, there is no one there to hold onto anything. It is not only the object of experience that is emptied, that is seen to be fundamentally nonexistent, even though it is experienced. The subject itself is emptied as well. Both experiencer and experienced are characterized by the fundamental absence of the absolute. There cannot be loss because there is nothing that can be lost.

The essential *nous* luminates now mostly with red and gold radiance, and perception becomes more precise and faceted. The insight that flashes out is that this coemergence of appearance and absolute resolves rapprochement.

> *This issue of rapprochement surfaces each time a new*
> *dimension of being is disclosed. It appears as a conflict*

between the presence of Being and the appearance of the world, between Being and the world. The conflict is the position that it is not possible to have both, not imaginable to experience both simultaneously, because of an apparent polarity. This polarity stems from the early relationship with one's mother, where one's sense of self was seen as antithetical to merging with her. So the individual soul grows up firmly believing that one can be either separate and independent, or merged and absorbed. In time, as the process of inner unfoldment deepens, the mother becomes the world and the sense of self is the presence of Being. At the level of the absolute the dichotomy appears as between the world as appearance and the emptiness of the absolute.

In the condition of coemergent presence, appearance and the absolute are totally coemergent, completely mixed and coextensive. Everything is absolutely inseparable from spaceless emptiness. The source of all manifestation is indistinguishable from all manifestation, including the individual soul.

Karen and I continue our discussion, laughing in delight, as we experience ourselves as translucent nonexistent souls sipping nonexistent hot tea from solid but totally transparent and weightless cups.

The face is God's face
The hand is the hand of the universe.
Where is the I?

Thirteen

Absolute Action

Even though realization of the absolute brings total contentment, its many mysteries continue to fire my curiosity. The coemergence of the soul with the absolute begins the realization of the coemergence of all manifestations. This in turn reveals the subtle relation between awareness and the absolute. My experience of the absolute has involved being a consciousness that apprehends it by touching it. The consciousness can be the clarified soul, or any aspect of essence. In this process the consciousness dissolves into its blackness, as it becomes aware of it as total nonbeing. Another way of experiencing the absolute is to be the absolute totally, aware of manifestation arising within it, an extension of it. In this condition awareness arises within the absolute as the ground of all manifestation, as luminosity or clarity.

Coemergence reveals that the awareness of the absolute is totally inseparable from its emptiness. Emptiness and awareness are two sides of the absolute, totally coemergent and inseparable. I cannot say that the absolute is clarity or luminosity, because it is much more. I cannot say it is simply emptiness, for it is so rich and so present. As the absolute I recognize myself as awareness which is presence, which is at the same time a lightness, an emptiness. My emptiness is my presence, and my presence is my awareness.

I see that the absolute has a luminosity, a clarity, but not the same as clear light or pure presence. Clear light is colorless, transparent luminosity, a very light and delicate presence. Pure presence is also colorless and transparent, but with a sense of fullness. These levels of consciousness can apprehend the absolute, and can be manifest by the absolute as the ground of all appearance. Yet the clarity and luminosity of the absolute are even subtler than these very subtle forms of consciousness. Its clarity and luminosity are implicit, not manifest. Its blackness is not the absence of light, but its source.

The inherent clarity of the absolute is prior to light. There is complete absence of obscurations. The fact that it is nonbeing makes it totally transparent, without this transparency appearing as clear light. But since, on the other hand, the absolute is not a vacant emptiness, but what truly is, this transparency becomes awareness. The awareness of its facticity is then inherent in the reality of its facticity.

This inherent clarity of the absolute is its own intrinsic knowingness. Its facticity is inherently knowing. I experience this knowing as an implicit clear light, not differentiated as clear light, but which can plumb the depths of the absolute. It is a clear consciousness completely inseparable from the absolute.

I experience the absolute as both knowable and unknowable. I can plumb its depths, and gain a great deal of experience and insight. I can describe what I experience in increasing detail, with more and more precision. But it is clear that the nature of this inexhaustible vastness allows no final or definitive knowledge. The absolute is knowable in that we can become aware of it; many poets and spiritual masters spent their lives talking and writing about it. It is unknowable in that our knowledge is endless and cannot be final. Its nature is indeterminable because it is inexhaustible.

The knowledge of the absolute always involves the revelations of the process of contemplating it, of experiencing it ever more deeply and clearly. It always involves a contemplating consciousness. The absolute is not absolutely alone. When there is no longer a contemplating consciousness, then there is no reflection on the absolute; there is only being it. Then there is no content that can be pointed to.

In other words, no fixed position or final conclusion can be taken regarding the absolute. To fully apprehend it is to know it as mystery.

A few days later...

The contemplation of the absolute continues with its own momentum, without my personal prompting. The consciousness finds itself in the mysterious blackness of the absolute, and a process of sensing into its depths spontaneously commences. I keep returning to this mystery, this intimacy, this delicacy, this contentment, this peace, this freedom, this infinity of release. The absolute cannot even be called space, even though it is a vastness. Ordinarily I see it as spacious. But as I plumb this spaciousness, it dissolves into a spaceless or dimensionless nothing. The result is absence, the opposite of existence. Then there is no sense of extension, and also no sense of no extension. Awareness of the absolute remains, but this awareness is free of the concept or sense of extension. In this subtle perception, knowingness borders on cessation.

The next day...

The absolute is indeterminate intimacy, the essence of Being. The sense of intimacy comes from the transparency coemergent with centerless knowingness: I am totally in touch with myself at each point of my presence, with no veils. In this complete in-touchness there is a sense of privacy, of interiority. This delicate interiority is the essence of intimacy. There is no subject being intimate with an object; in fact there is nothing to be intimate with. Intimacy is merely the condition of total in-touchness.

The absolute is definitely Being, but it cannot be said to be existence, or even presence. It is Being in that there is an actuality that we do encounter. In fact, it is the only certain being; everything else arises out of it, and is transitory. However, this beingness of the absolute is devoid of the concept or feeling of existence, empty of the concept or sense of presence. There is an immediacy of self-awareness, but there is nothing to say about what the awareness is aware of. I sometimes call it absolute Being.

Realizing that the absolute is Being, even though there is no sense or idea of existence, can be problematic. The mind tends to objectify being, even absolute being. If something exists in any mode, the mind seems to be impelled to view it as an object, as an independent existent. It is almost impossible in most conditions of mind to think or talk about something without reifying it. The very word "something" contains "thing" which the mind inevitably associates with what it perceives as separate entities. We may think about, or even talk about, the absolute; but it cannot be objectified without ending up with something else. To objectify the absolute is to delimit it, and then it is not the absolute anymore.

The absolute is not something other than the consciousness that contemplates it. It is not something outside of the awareness that inquires into it. It is not a product of consciousness or perception, but their very source. It is also not a percept that can be delineated completely. In fact, it is not a percept, even though we seem to have the experience of perceiving it. It is the ground of all perception, all experience. And this ground is paradoxically not only nonexistent, it is nonexistence. This nonexistence is also mysteriously inseparable from all existence, as its ultimate truth and reality. The absolute is what gives everything its existence, without it itself being an existent.

A few days later...

In the morning meditation I become aware of a vague dissatisfaction. I remain mostly in nonconceptual abiding in the absolute, but something seems to be percolating. I go to the office, begin seeing students, and work as usual. Gradually the vague discontent becomes clearer. I begin to feel a deep sadness, almost a longing. I realize at some point that even though I am doing well working, I feel that I do not want to work. Inquiring into this feeling, I see it is not only about working, but about activity in general.

I do not want to do anything. Not only that, the insight arises that I do not want to be part of manifestation. I want to be quiet and inactive. I want to be still, not involved in any activity.

As I stay with this thread without taking a position regarding the feelings, I realize I want to be a silent and passive witness of everything, without participating. I want to be aware of the mystery of the absolute, and I do not want to be separated from it.

As long as I am not too active, I am the absolute or an inseparable part of it. However, when there is personal functioning I become involved, for example, when I interact with students on a level they can relate to, and manifest what they need. As personal functioning dominates the absolute recedes, and I experience some separation from it. I become a functioning person, and am no longer totally immersed in the intimacy. Here is where deep sadness arises; it is about the separation from the absolute, and leads to the feeling of longing to be reunited with the absolute.

I begin to wonder whether this separation is necessary. I begin to see that there remains a lack of complete integration. I have mostly experienced the soul integrated into the absolute in various degrees. I can see now that the process of integration has not yet included the functioning of the soul. The possibility now appears of being the absolute and witnessing the person who is working. When this happens, I see myself as the absolute witness behind and beyond all happening. Yet this does not seem to be the integration I feel is missing.

The issue seems to be a form of the rapprochement conflict. I love being the absolute transcendence, but I also love being personally with others, and working with students in a personal way. So the issue is a conflict between two loves, between witnessing and personal involvement.

The next afternoon…

After finishing work, I am moving around in the yard, looking at the flowers and watching the birds fly between trees.

I am aware of the mysterious depth of the absolute as my center, but I realize it is not only the center of my experience. It is the center of my movement; in fact my movement seems to be inseparable from the depths. My movements, and my functioning in general, manifest as part of the lumination of this absolute stillness.

The variegated radiance of the absolute manifests at my physical locus as a flow inseparable from movement. I experience the silence and stillness of the absolute as the center of experience, and the soul as a flow of changes, movements and functioning. More accurately, the movement and functioning appear as fluctuations in the flow of consciousness that is the soul. The stillness and silence are coemergent with the flow. This indicates the integration of the soul's functioning with the absolute. The absolute emptiness is so completely united with the flowing consciousness of the soul that the visual effect is that the movements are very subtle luminations of the absolute. At my locus the black vastness seems to flow with a dynamic luminosity. The absolute displays not only an inherent luminosity but also a magical dynamism.

Few days later...

The integration of individual functioning in the absolute is becoming a continuing realization, a station. When I am relaxed, working or doing any practice, I find myself in this peaceful stillness that is inseparable from appearance and functioning. I am the absolute stillness, and at the same time personally functioning, acting and interacting. The experience is mostly of personal functioning, and not boundless functioning. I am only occasionally aware of all of appearance as a luminous flow from the stillness.

The movement is smooth and light, free and spontaneous. The body is as light as light. It is a dynamic luminosity. Functioning is easy and complete, and totally in the moment. In this state, when I act I am aware of a formless and mysterious nothingness that acts by varying its external forms. I move the hand, but I am formless boundless nothing, moving a form that is inseparable from this nothingness. The movement is nothing but the flow of shifting forms through which the mysterious depth manifests.

I am stillness, yet I am movement. My movement is the flow of my stillness. The flow is nothing but my dynamic radiance. With all my dynamism, the origin of all change and movement, I never cease being absolute stillness.

The face of the ancient one
Can only love
Another face of his.

Fourteen

Life and the Deathless

One day I become aware of a subtle contraction of the mobius center at the sternum. Being subtle, it does not affect my sense of presence or my capacity to function. Retaining this impression in my awareness in the course of the day's activities, I realize at some point that it is part of a larger condition. I become aware of a small hole at the location of the solar plexus. My interest is stimulated; I have not experienced a hole in this location for a long time. An easy, spontaneous inquiry into this experience arises.

The light-hearted inquiry intensifies the throbbing at the center of the forehead. The throbbing has a sense of quietness and peace, a radiating stillness. I see the essential *nous*, the discriminating intelligence or diamond guidance, mostly black. A black presence of stillness glimmers with faceted radiance, as it is activated by the curiosity and questioning.

The contraction at the mobius relaxes and dissolves, and sadness and emptiness arise. The sadness develops into deep black tears. The tears are deep and warm, and seem to drench the totality of my inner conscious field. The sense of teary sadness comes and goes; I realize there is some difficulty in staying with the experience. This intensifies my curiosity, and adds a silvery glimmer to the diamond blackness of the *nous*, expressing steadfastness in inquiry.

The sadness deepens and becomes more definite. This increases my awareness of the depth and intimacy of blackness. My consciousness is pervaded by the blackness of the absolute, as I relax into its depth, enfolded by intimacy, soft and light, peaceful and exquisite. My center of awareness sinks deeper into the intimate depths, with a visual sense of receding away from the surface awareness of the environment. I am now centered in a depth from which all of existence appears as surface. It is similar to being in the depths of an ocean, perceiving the changing phenomena at its surface. As I recede into this depth, the issues related to the teary sadness are revealed.

Since the discovery of the absolute some years ago, and its eventual realization, I have been dealing with the issue of a certain death, as I contemplate my eventual physical death.

I have been thinking about death for years now, aware of its presence and contemplating its truth. I have wondered, with an innocent mind, what death means, what it might feel like, and how I feel about it. This contemplation and inquiry have intensified recently because of some health problems that have made me more aware of the vulnerability of the physical body. The sadness, in conjunction with the intimate depth of the absolute, makes it clear now that there is something about death I have not come to terms with. It is not fear, not pain, not fear of the unknown. It is not a concern about the death of the self, or about the cessation of consciousness. I have experienced these forms of death, but these experiences have not completely fulfilled my contemplation of death. A question still remains, along with a deep, teary sadness.

The black *nous* glimmers now with a radiant pearly sheen, as it throbs at the location of the forehead. The realization arises that the sadness is about a certain kind of aloneness, different from the sorts of aloneness I have known. There is a concern, almost a fear, but this fear is not about being totally alone. It is not exactly the state of aloneness that I feel sad about. It is rather the recognition that physical death will mean leaving my life, leaving all that I cherish in this life. Understanding fills the consciousness:

Death is the loss of personal life.

This loss has implications I have never fully come to terms with. Death is no longer living this particular present life. It is my particular, present life that I will leave, and not only life in general. This is not a philosophical question; it is a completely personal concern. The sadness is the grief about recognizing that I cannot remain with what I love. When physical death arrives, I will lose contact with all that I have come to love in this world.

Death will be the end of contact with family, friends, students, places, things, activities, work; everything and everyone I love and cherish. I will no longer experience the everyday simple things of life; sleeping, eating, showering, making love, conversation, the sky, the mountains, the grass, the birds, colors and flavors, and so on. I will no longer converse with Marie at the breakfast table. I will no longer watch and listen to the birds. I will no longer experience physical touch and its warmth. It will not be possible to go for a drive with my friend Karen, or have a discussion with my friend Ron, or go out to dinner with friends and family. All impressions of life will leave me. I feel the grief and the tears, as I acknowledge this inevitable and unavoidable loss, especially the loss of the manifestations I have come to love, those that have become dear to me.

The poignant understanding sinks very deep: the concern is not fear of annihilation. It is not fear of loss of essence or Being. It is the anticipation of loss of the world, estrangement from the world I know and love. I see that in the first half of my life, before the awakening and transformation, I had a schizoid distance, and indifference, towards life and its simple happenings. I did not deeply care about life, and my love was limited. But for some years, the inner transformation has steadily diminished this distance from my world, and my appreciation of this world has become increasingly intimate. I have gradually become more fully involved, more into life and people and happenings. Love and pleasure have deepened and expanded in many ways, and in many areas. I realize that I have not only been more involved in life, but enjoying with increasing passion and fullness the particulars of my life.

The involvement, intimacy and enjoyment have been actually much deeper than I have allowed myself to recognize. I have been mostly preoccupied with the exploration of the beautiful and exquisite manifestations of Being, and have not explicitly discerned the deepening involvement, love and enjoyment of life that this exploration allowed. But as I acknowledge it, and feel it, I am confronted with the possibility of losing it when I physically die.

The insight illuminates the mind, as the *nous* radiates bright yellow and orange: I have not completely and explicitly acknowledged the fullness of the life I have been living, the depth of love and completeness of enjoyment, because of the fear of losing it. Fully enjoying living, I have come face to face with the reality of death. And I see that to consciously enjoy this fullness of life I must fully and consciously accept death.

I still feel that I do not want to leave the people and the things that I love. This refusal becomes a contraction of the soul, a tightening at the mobius. The hole at the solar plexus indicates the loss of will and choice as I recognize the impossibility of holding on to my present life. I cannot deny the certain eventuality of death. As the contraction lets go slowly, and in spite of me, due to the inexorable pressure of truth, I see myself as the blackness of the absolute receding from the individual soul. I start experiencing myself as the intimacy of the absolute, and the soul as only a surface manifestation. The totality of the life of the soul appears now as a luminous, colorful ripple arising in the vastness of the mystery.

I realize that this is the place from which to confront death. As the absolute I recognize myself as the deathless. And from this place there is serenity about death, and about the separation from loved ones. In contrast, from the vantage point of the contracted soul death is very undesirable and threatening.

Understanding now focuses on the last half of my life. It seems that as I enjoy life and become more fully involved in it, certain deep and hitherto unknown tendencies begin to manifest. The intimate involvement with life and its particulars subtly focuses my attention on this dimension of experience, and my awareness of the depth of ipseity begins to recede. Life can become all-consuming, the only reality. In subtle, unconscious ways I lose balance, and love becomes attachment. This tends to separate the soul from the absolute, and create a dichotomy between life and death.

Clearly, in this process I am dealing with the separation of soul from absolute, and their reintegration. I still somehow go from one to the other, even though I have had numerous, powerful experiences of integration, have developed a deep experiential understanding of their nonduality, and have actualized a steadily deepening coemergence.

The integration of soul and absolute is becoming necessary as I confront death. It seems that besides the overriding love of truth, love of life has motivated me to seek truth. Now I have life, and it is good. This motivation is not as strong now. However, not being able to forget or deny death is challenging me at a new depth, making it necessary for me to seek further truth. Love of life is still present, and it is one important reason why I am concerned about death. In the past, life has impelled me to inquire; now death is doing the impelling.

A few days later…

I am in a meeting, teaching a small group the experience and perspective of the universal witness. As usual, the witness space arises in the room, but I notice that my experience of it is now different from what I remember from a few years before. I experience myself as both the depth of the absolute and the witnessing space simultaneously. In fact, I realize here that the universal witness is nothing but a limited way of experiencing the absolute as identity. Now I am the luminous black depth, but as a silent witness. The sheer awareness and silence fill the room, as many of the students begin to share in the experience of pure witnessing.

The meeting is over and I leave the room with my close friend, Karen. We walk from the meeting hall towards my room, which is in a nearby building. It is night, darkness all around us, and brilliant stars fill the heavens. It is somewhat cool on this spring night, and I can smell the earth and the trees on both sides of us. Silence pervades everything, even though we are talking. It is as if the earth is in deep sleep.

As we are leisurely walking and talking, the sense is that I am walking, but I am also watching myself walking. I am a personal presence, a fullness that is an extension of the black absolute mystery, walking on the road with Karen. At the same time, I am the absolute vastness, as the background of all appearance, witnessing my personal presence walking. Karen is experiencing herself the same way. We are personal presences, both coemergent with, and inseparable extensions from, the mysterious vastness of the absolute. At the same time, we are each this black vastness witnessing the two of us walking.

There is the perception of appearance as surface. But this surface, which is all that perception beholds, is three dimensional and dynamic. The darkness of the night and the luminous blackness of the absolute are almost indistinguishable. This mysterious blackness projects itself dynamically as the various forms, hills and trees, buildings and cars, stars and lights. My personal presence, inseparable from the body, and that of Karen, are parts of this dynamic appearance, but inseparable from it. We are both in oneness with all of existence. At the same time, our personal presences are clearly inseparable extensions of the black absolute into this oneness of appearance. We recognize that each of us is a projection of the absolute mystery as a personal presence walking into the appearance, an appearance that the absolute is also projecting. As we talk it is really the absolute talking to himself, while he walks as two people.

I am both a dynamic embodied presence and a transcendent witnessing background, simultaneously. These manifestations are completely coemergent. The experience is very mysterious, and totally confounding to the mind.

The insight arises that this condition is the resolution of the issue I have been working on for several years, the issue of the dichotomy between life and death, soul and absolute. I am both the soul as an embodied dynamic presence, and the vastness of the witnessing absolute. I am the soul as an expression and extension of the absolute, while remaining the transcendent absolute. I am fully the personal soul, and I am completely the absolute vastness. Fullness, absence and mystery are all present.

Karen bids me good night as we reach my room. Entering, I am aware of bringing the luminous darkness into the room, along with my personal presence. The whole room, the furniture, the lights, all constitute a graceful, exquisite manifestation of my vastness, as my personal presence inhabits and moves within it.

The Diamond Approach^{SM} is taught by Ridhwan teachers, certified by the Ridhwan Foundation. Ridhwan teachers are also ordained ministers of the Ridhwan Foundation. They are trained by DHAT Institute, the educational arm of the Ridhwan Foundation, through an extensive seven-year program, which is in addition to their work and participation as students of the Diamond Approach^{SM}. The certification process ensures that each person has a good working understanding of the Diamond Approach^{SM} and a sufficient capacity to teach it before being ordained and authorized to be a Ridhwan teacher.

The Diamond Approach^{SM} described in this book is taught in group and private settings in California and Colorado by Ridhwan teachers.

For information, write:

> Ridhwan
> P.O. Box 10114
> Berkeley, California 94709-5114

> Ridhwan School
> P.O. Box 18166
> Boulder, Colorado 80308–8166

Satellite groups operate in other national and international locations. For information about these groups, or to explore starting a group in your area, taught by certified Ridhwan teachers, write:

> Ridhwan
> P.O. Box 10114
> Berkeley, California 94709-5114